I0709728

Praise for
Play You, The Role of a Lifetime

"Great actors transform a script into something unforgettable. Pam Sherman shows you how to do the same with your life and your career."
—Marshall Goldsmith, PhD, Thinkers50 #1 Executive Coach and *New York Times* Bestselling Author

"Pam Sherman shows how to bring your whole self to every room you enter, so you can make a greater impact. *Play You, The Role of a Lifetime,* is both a pep talk and a practical guide for stepping into your full power."
—Dorie Clark, Executive Education Faculty at Columbia Business School and *Wall Street Journal* Bestselling Author of *The Long Game*

"Connectional intelligence is about unlocking value in our relationships. Pam Sherman's *Play You, The Role of a Lifetime* gives us the tools to close the believability gap—making every connection more meaningful and impactful."
—Erica Dhawan, Keynote Speaker and Bestselling Author of *Digital Body Language*

"In *Play You, The Role of a Lifetime,* Pam Sherman offers a compelling guide to stepping into your most courageous, connected self. On these pages, you will learn how to live and lead with presence and purpose."
—Alexandra H. Solomon, PhD, Bestselling Author of *Love Every Day* and Host of the podcast, *Reimagining Love*

"Anyone on-air knows acting techniques give you the discipline to create authenticity. Pam Sherman knows and shows us how the two can meld perfectly."
—Dan Patrick, Host of *The Dan Patrick Show*

"Play You, The Role of a Lifetime is like a reassuring hug for anyone who has grappled with the tension between authenticity and what is required to get the job done. Pam Sherman reassures us that this high wire act isn't all in our heads and then offers incisive coaching and exercises that help us cultivate self-awareness and extend the value of believability far beyond our professional lives."

—Alicia Menendez, Journalist and Bestselling Author
of *The Likability Trap*

"If you've ever struggled to feel like 'yourself' in high-stakes moments, *Play You, The Role of a Lifetime* is the answer. Pam Sherman offers a fresh, accessible way to use your voice, own the room, and connect with others in a way that truly lands."

—Tasha Eurich, PhD, Organizational Psychologist
and Bestselling Author of *Shatterproof,*
Insight,* and *Bankable Leadership

"Play You, The Role of a Lifetime is a guide for showing up—even when it's hard. Pam offers practical wisdom about leading with confidence even when your inner critic is loud."

—Morra Aarons-Mele, Bestselling Author
of *The Anxious Achiever*

"Believability changes everything—it's the gap between influence and invisibility. *Play You, The Role of a Lifetime* shows you how to claim it, own it, and use it to lead with a power that is fully your own."

—Deepa Purushothaman, Bestselling Author
of *The First, the Few, the Only*

"As someone who has spent her lifetime helping people forge meaningful connections, I found *Play You, The Role of a Lifetime* to be a powerful guide for showing up and making every moment count."

—Susan McPherson, Author of *The Lost Art of Connecting*

"In *Play You, The Role of a Lifetime,* Pam Sherman delivers a compelling guide to bridging the gap between how you see yourself and how others experience you. With warmth, wit, and wisdom, she shows how the thing people respond to most—our whole, true self—is often the very thing we're least sure how to express. Pam offers clear, practical insights and tools that will help you build trust, connection, and believability in work and life."
> **—Karen Eber, Author of *The Perfect Story*, TED Speaker, and leadership and culture Expert**

"*Play You, The Role of a Lifetime* is a powerful guide to bridging the gap between who we are and how we lead—with presence, purpose, and humanity."
> **—Erica Keswin, Workplace Strategist and Bestselling Author of *Bring Your Human to Work***

"*Play You, The Role of a Lifetime* is the perfect antidote to imposter syndrome. The surprising solution? Think like an actor. The best actors focus on the aspects of their role that align with their true self and allow them to shine. Packed with practical strategies and unexpected insights, this book will help boost your confidence in every role you play."
> **—Ron Friedman, PhD, Bestselling Author of *Superteams* and *The Best Place to Work***

"Connection isn't accidental—it's intentional. In *Play You, The Role of a Lifetime*, Pam Sherman reveals the tools we all need to make our relationships more authentic, fulfilling, and best of all, reciprocal."
> **—Allison Gilbert, Bestselling Coauthor of *The Joy of Connections***

PLAY YOU

THE ROLE OF A LIFETIME

Bridge the Believability Gap to Boost Your Confidence, Connection, and Impact

PAM SHERMAN

With Lari Bishop

Post Hill PRESS

A POST HILL PRESS BOOK
ISBN: 979-8-89565-020-2
ISBN (eBook): 979-8-89565-021-9

Play You, the Role of a Lifetime:
Bridge the Believability Gap to Boost Your Confidence, Connection, and Impact

Cover design by Sheila Parr

EDGE: Explore, Dream, Grow & Excite® is a registered trademark of Business Advantage, Inc.

Post Hill Press
New York • Nashville
posthillpress.com

Published in the United States of America
1 2 3 4 5 6 7 8 9 10

To NES, ZBS, ERS.

And to all my fellow players.

CONTENTS

CHAPTER 1

BRIDGING THE BELIEVABILITY GAP

"To be believable we must be credible; to be credible we must be truthful."[1]—EDWARD R. MURROW

When I met Ben for the first time, I felt like I was watching someone read from a script titled "Leader." And clearly, he had written that script based on dysfunctional, domineering leadership he had experienced in toxic cultures. At least, that's what reviews from his colleagues, his team, and his bosses indicated. Their comments read like the worst opening night pan from a theater critic: Ben was cold, aggressive, difficult, even mean.

That wasn't the kind of character the executive team wanted in their play. It wasn't a character that would ever fit into their culture. I had been brought in to help Ben…adjust.

Here's the thing—that character they all described was *not* the guy I met. The Ben I met might have been reading from a script, but he was also open to working with me and interested in improving. Yes, he was reserved, but he also told me he loved his job, the company, and his team. If I had told Ben's team that he loved them, I would be laughed off the metaphorical stage. And *he* sure as heck wasn't going to tell them.

When I asked him what he thought about the review comments, he said, "I was just trying to be an effective leader." But he also told me it was hard to make things happen, to achieve goals, to get his team on board. Of course it was! The leader he was showing up as was not his true character. It was a kind of costume he put on or character archetype he held himself up against: the hard-hearted leader. And he was feeling the consequences.

I could relate to Ben, to the struggle of trying to be somebody other than who you are at your core. When I was a little girl, I would play the piano with the door of our house wide open hoping that a wandering talent agent would hear me and cast me on Broadway. The first problem with my plan was that agents don't wander the streets of Staten Island. The second was that I can't sing. The third was that I came from a very conservative family. My dad was a gynecologist, and my mother was a psychoanalyst. If I had a headache my dad would tell me to take two aspirin, and my mom would ask me who I was mad at. To them, being an actor was akin to being an axe murderer. So even though I double majored in theater and international relations in college (I used to tell my peers that my tap dancing classes would make me a better diplomat), I put my acting dreams away—and became a lawyer.

I thought the work would be like the lawyering I'd seen on TV. But instead of incendiary courtroom battles, I was sitting on the floor surrounded by law texts or boxes of accounting reports. Instead of wordsmithing killer arguments, I was chasing down court clerks. I was miserable. I would shut my door for ten or fifteen minutes in the middle of the day, lie on the floor, and silently scream at the ceiling.

But the real problem wasn't the gap between what I thought the work would be and what it actually was. The real problem was that I had a picture in my head of what a *lawyer* should be—and it wasn't me. I felt like I was wearing an ill-fitting suit. Actually, I *was* wearing ill-fitting suits—with shoulder pads and brooches at the neck. Blech. I thought these costumes would help. They didn't. My confidence was slipping away, I was less creative, and I was having a hard time holding my own with my colleagues, clients, and the all-important partners. And that's *definitely* not me.

Both Ben and I spent way too much time worrying about what people thought of us in our roles, playing to assumptions and stereotypes, instead of focusing on how we were uniquely qualified to deliver what they *needed* from us. We didn't believe in ourselves, and we weren't believable to others, either.

We were stuck in the believability gap. It's the gap between who we fundamentally are and who we think we are expected to be, which makes us less believable to ourselves. And it's the gap between who we fundamentally are and how we show up for other people, which makes us less believable to them.

To be successful and fulfilled in almost any role—whether it's engineer, customer service team lead, community organizer, parent, or executive vice president of institutional banking—you have to overcome both.

I discovered how when I began planning my escape from the world of law and pursued my first love. I signed up for an acting class after work to bring some joy back into my life and find a place where I could be "the real me." I dove into the work of trying to understand who my characters were at their core, what they had to contribute to the story and the important moments on the stage, and how to portray them truthfully, believably, to all the people in the room or theater—the audience, the director, the other actors creating the imagined world with me.

And the most surprising thing happened. In a rehearsal studio, working with great teachers, I found a way to stop pretending! I began to realize a counterintuitive truth: to be more believable in the rest of my life, to climb out the believability gap I was in, I could turn to the tools the most compelling actors use to create believable, compelling characters, to build connection with their audiences, and to have a greater impact.

I'm not talking about being disingenuous. I'm not talking about putting on a better mask. My favorite definition of acting comes from the wonderful teacher Sanford Meisner, who said, "Acting is the ability to behave absolutely truthfully under the imaginary circumstances."[2] When we're being truthful and genuine in our given real-life circumstances, we're more believable to ourselves and others.

Why does being believable matter in today's world, when it can feel like showing up truthfully seems to matter less and less in our increasingly virtual lives? Or why am I not writing about authenticity instead? First, when we're able to bring our whole selves to a situation—online or IRL (in real life)—with transparency and honesty, we feel more confident. And we stand out just by being our true, wonderful, unique selves. Second, we're able to build connections and "make things happen," to use Ben's words. Being believable is a generous interplay that requires us to acknowledge the other people on stage with us, trying to play their roles effectively, and the story we're creating together. Authenticity might help us find some inner truth, but if we don't take it further and bring that truth to the world to be more believable to and with others, we miss opportunities to contribute to and make progress in that story.

The bottom line is that believability is the path to confidence, connection, and impact. In today's world, all three matter to our wellbeing, our success, our happiness and fulfillment. Working on your truthful believability allows you to bring more of who you are at your core alive in the world, to shine your glorious rays out toward others, to discover the internal power you carry to improve your own life and have a positive impact on those around you and the world at large.

That's what I want to help you achieve in your work and life. This book is for you if you're trying to show up every day and make a difference, make progress, advocate for your ideas, bring people on board, or advance faster in your career. Maybe you're early in your career and are trying to show up comfortable and confident in a new role. Maybe you're an engineer who's finding out that dropping a report on somebody's desk and darting out of the room isn't how you get more funding for your project. Maybe you're a lawyer who needs to reveal your passion for a client's cause to win more cases and bring in more revenue. Or maybe you need to share your expertise, or even step onto an actual stage, but fear of being in the spotlight is holding you back.

Regardless of your struggle, I'll help by giving you "permission" and techniques for bringing more of yourself to any role, so that you can behave truthfully and believably. As we go, I'll examine the things that can widen the believability gap, internal and external, so you can spot where you might have work to do. I'll help you clarify who you are at your core, where you're headed, and what obstacles are keeping you from making progress along your personal story arc. And I'll boost your courage and confidence so you can take those important steps into the spotlight and connect powerfully with the people you most want to impact, influence, or lead.

So if you're ready to be who you are, wherever you are, in order to energize yourself and ignite your audiences—of one or one thousand—this book is for you.

How Believability Grows Our Confidence, Connection, and Impact

Not long ago, I had a conversation that illustrates perfectly why I'm writing this book. I interviewed the boss of a new client, Mara. Mara hadn't been in her management role long. She had the right experience, though, because she had been working in her department for a few years—which was the source of her problem! You could see her trying to prove she was worthy of the promotion— but it was like watching a high school play that was so awkward and self-conscious you wanted to rush for the exit. Her boss captured the issue perfectly, saying, "You know, the problem is that she thinks she has to act like the last guy."

The problem of believability crops up for all of us, especially when we either think who we are isn't enough, or isn't "right for the role," or when the culture makes it feel high-risk to show up as ourselves.

Let's look a little closer at that second problem first, which unfortunately, you may have experienced. Toxic cultures, where people feel that who they fundamentally are doesn't matter and isn't valued, are stressful and dysfunctional. Organizational researcher Patricia Faison Hewlin found that people who think they have to suppress their personal values on the job experience more symptoms of depression and stress. Their mental and physical well-being take the hit.[3] And surprise, surprise, those companies have a hard time holding onto their employees. When PwC did a survey of more than 50,000 employees around the world, they found that one of the big differences between people who were thinking about leaving and people who weren't was whether they felt they could "truly be themselves at work."[4]

Which brings us back to the first problem. Even in healthy cultures, many of us are struggling to bridge the believability gap, and especially the internal gap, which has existed since humans became conscious. But it has been made worse in new and improved ways by our modern world. With hybrid workplaces, our lives can feel on display, exposed, and up for scrutiny. On social media, we're constantly comparing ourselves to everybody else who's living their "best life." And the general media overload of stories about people who seem to be miraculously nailing it—or at least doing better than you—can actually trigger your brain to feel threatened and want to engage in "fight or flight." The human brain processes perceived social threats in many of the same ways that it processes physical threats.

The result? We feel so much pressure to match a cardboard cutout for each role we play, in our professional and personal lives. We're overwhelmed by expectations, underconfident in our ability to meet them, and afraid of being discovered as a fraud, especially when we have to step into the spotlight, metaphorically or literally. To be credible and valued, we think we have to do one of two things: diminish who we are or exaggerate it. In the first case, we extinguish our light every day by showing up as somebody other than the character at our core, and that can be truly soul sucking. Or we exaggerate elements of that character to fulfill some ideal of who we think we're *supposed* to be. Just look at Ben. Could he be some of the things he was accused of in his review? Sure, sometimes. But most of the time? That was him exaggerating an aspect of his personality that he thought would make him an ideal leader.

I fell into the "diminishment" camp. And I had to find a way to release my inner me, or I was going to implode. Within a few months of getting back into the acting studio, my transformation was kind of miraculous. The work I was doing in class to explore characters, to dream of more possibilities, and to use my energy and passion to excite audiences was helping me rediscover who I truly was, what I valued, and what I had to offer. At work, I became more confident and…powerful. I stood up for myself more (especially when I was getting yelled at by one of the partners). I trusted my instincts and communicated more naturally. I became a better advocate for my clients. I even started to dress differently—far fewer brooches. And…I was more in demand than ever by clients and colleagues! As I led my double life, running between depositions for clients and auditions for commercials, I felt myself become more truthful and believable—and that shift led to a life that has been full of excitement, fulfillment, connection, and impact.

We're facing a pivotal moment in human history—a moment that requires us to double down on *being* human. In his future forward book *Humans Are Underrated*, published more than ten years ago, Geoff Colvin wrote, "The meaning of great performance has changed. It used to be that you had to be good at being machine-like. Now, increasingly, you have to be good at being a person. Great performance requires us to be intensely human beings."[5] With the advent of AI, the impact of social media and our increasingly virtual communication, and the general pace of change in life and in work, we're facing an onslaught of forces that can pull us away from what really empowers us in the world: being our true core selves to build connection and have a powerful impact. This makes the work of closing the believability gap, and showing up as fully, truthfully, wholly human, more important than ever. It's how we'll stand out from the crowd, how we'll leverage our humanity to be more powerful in the world, and I believe it's how each of us can contribute to a better, more generous world.

And in your day-to-day life, growing your believability will lessen your stress, grow your confidence, help you create deeper and more fulfilling connections and relationships, and expand your influence and impact. It will empower you to create the life and career you want, within your ever-changing circumstances.

How Acting Techniques Can Help Us Be Our Truthful Selves

It's not news that we're *supposed* to be self-aware and authentic and vulnerable. Most of us understand innately that when we can be our amazing true selves, transparently, our work lives and personal lives become easier and full of more possibility. But we don't always know how to make it happen. What we're missing are actionable, insight-generating exercises and strategies that can help us "behave truthfully" in any circumstance. That's what acting techniques are all about. They can help you understand the core of your character, the source of your greatest strength. They can help you align that character with whatever role you're playing and then leverage it to draw people into your story.

And yes, I get that that the solution I'm offering for becoming more believable as *you* seems like a contradiction because it comes from a profession known for convincingly playing somebody else. But I've seen the power of doing the courageous work I'll describe in this book over the last two decades as I've worked with people all over the world as a leadership, team performance, and communication consultant. Whether I'm working with managers, C-suite executives, or teams at Fortune 50 companies, I've seen the impact it has on how people show up, how they work together, their results, how they take on new challenges and opportunities, and how they feel every day.

It was an interesting journey to get there myself, though. I eventually left the world of law to become an actor full time. That sounds like a crazy statement to some people, which is why I was included in a story in *People* magazine about people ditching their day jobs to follow their passions. I was a professional actor for ten years—you may have even seen me off-off-Broadway (a.k.a. Staten Island and Queens), at the Kennedy Center, or in an episode of *Homicide: Life on the Street.*

One day, the head of training for a government antitrust department saw the article in *People*, got in touch, and asked, essentially, "Can you help my attorneys be more interesting?" My first thought was, *Antitrust attorneys? No.* But then I considered what she was really asking: Can you help them be more persuasive, credible, believable? *That's all acting is,* I thought. So I did my best to translate the techniques I relied on for their needs—and it worked incredibly well. I helped them show up with genuine passion and commitment to their cause. And I discovered that leading them on that journey combined so much of what I love about acting with an even stronger connection to and impact on my audience.

From there, one opportunity showed up after another because of how people talked about the experience of learning to be more wholly, truthfully believable. Year by year, I have proven the importance and possibilities of building believability through acting techniques.

A few years ago, I even went through the somewhat terrifying and grueling process of reproving and reconnecting with those techniques. After thirteen years away from the stage, I accepted an offer to play iconic humor columnist Erma Bombeck in the one-woman show, *Erma Bombeck: At Wit's End*, in theaters around the country. It was a leap of courage that offered important reminders about how to craft a character—a hero of mine—to be believable to me and others, how to take in feedback from a director, and even how to iron (wrinkle free shirts didn't exist in Erma's day). It has been the most enlightening, gratifying, and revealing journey, and it inspired this book.

Based on my years of experience as a coach and studying different acting approaches—from Stanislavski to Strasberg to Meisner to Chekhov—here's how I've translated the fundamentals:

- ★ *Explore* your character, your role, and your presence.
- ★ *Dream*, craft, and share your full story, the throughline of your backstory, and the story you're envisioning for the future.
- ★ *Grow* beyond your believability derailers—the thinking and behaviors keeping you from bringing your true self to the role you're currently playing.
- ★ *Excite* your audience—so that your message can have the impact you want it to have, whether you're talking to one person or one thousand.

It's the same journey actors go on as they take on a new role: learning about a character deeply, exploring the character's full story, rehearsing so that they can grow beyond the hurdles keeping them from bringing that character to life truthfully and believably, and then delivering an exciting performance that creates connection and impact.

Ben was a perfect example. I started at the beginning and helped him clarify who he was at his core and how he wanted to show up for his team, not the archetype he thought he should play. The more we talked, the more obvious it became that the pressure he put on himself to succeed didn't leave much time or room for self-reflection. He also thought to lead meant getting results, which meant being commanding. Who cares how anyone feels as long as the work gets done, right? Behind the archetype, though, was a passionate and caring person who wanted others to have the same opportunities he had. When he shared his backstory with me, it was clear why. He had been raised by a single mom in an impoverished neighborhood in Miami. He was driven and had earned a full scholarship, becoming the first in his family to go to college. For his whole adult life, he had volunteered with organizations that support students with backgrounds like his.

Ben's true character and his story were inspiring, but he wasn't bringing them to life in his role! One of his big beliefs was generosity, and that wasn't shining through. Once he saw that, we could talk about how to align his communication and behavior with who he is at his core, to have a positive impact. As Ben did the work, his presence shifted. He was more relaxed and open. He started talking with people in the office instead of sitting behind his closed door, only emerging from the wings to tell someone what to do. And by the next review cycle, Ben had become one of the biggest cheerleaders for the organization and his team. Honestly, it was one of the most profound turnarounds I've seen in my work. People trusted him more because he was more credible and transparent. He was closing the believability gap.

Your Journey Through This Book

The best actors close the believability gap by taking the audience on a powerful journey. That's my goal with this book. I'll walk you through the process and exercises I use in my personal and professional development work. I'll share truthful stories from my clients and from the world of acting, about the actor's process and what we can learn from it.

This book is constructed like a four-act play. In Part 1, we're introduced to the main character. In Part 2, we learn more about their dreams and story. In Part 3, we explore how they overcome the obstacles they're facing, internal and external. And in Part 4, we see how they step onto the stage of life as their whole, true self to impact others and the world around them. It's a compelling story and character arc—*your* compelling arc, because the main character in this play is you!

In Part 1, I'll start by helping you get to know yourself deeply—because you have to overcome any internal believability gap before you can tackle external believability gaps. If you can't be believable to yourself, you can't be believable to other people. And your genuine power comes from knowing your true self fully, not who you'd like to be or who others expect you to be.

You'll choose and articulate your Power Words—the few words that define who you are at your core, what drives you, what fuels your energy and passion. You'll learn that the clues about how to bring your true character to life come not only from within, but also from analyzing the script for the role you need to play—an essential technique for actors. And then you'll explore how to align your physical presence, especially your energy, voice and body language, with who you are at the core and the demands of the role you're playing.

In Part 2, you'll learn that to put your character out into the world believably, you need to share the grounding, revealing stories that have made you who you are and the inspiring, motivating stories about where you'll go from here—what your vision for the future is and how it connects with the throughline from your past. I'll help you become a story thinker and a story sharer. We'll explore what stories to share and how to develop and share them powerfully to build connection and encourage others to come on your journey with you.

In Part 3, we'll dive into your believability derailers, the thought patterns and behaviors that pull you away from your true character. Think about how Ben and I both struggled because we held onto stereotypical character archetypes—for me, the "made-for-TV lawyer," and for Ben, the "hard-ass boss"—rather than play our truthful selves. You'll learn the signs and symptoms of common archetypes and the negative scripts they spawn. And you'll learn strategies for rehearsing you. Most of us have suppressed aspects of our character for so long that it takes practice to feel comfortable bringing it to life through our behavior. And that can be especially true when we're working with a team, where we need to build trust.

In Part 4, I'll help you break the fourth wall, connect with your audience, and deliver your message with impact. Breaking the fourth wall refers to a character on stage or screen breaking out of the "room" they're in and addressing the audience directly. It can be a powerful way to connect with the audience, overcome apathy, and create transcendent moments. Any of us can do the same, from one-on-one conversations to speaking gigs in front of thousands of people. It starts with understanding your audience, their needs and wants, so that you can make *them* feel like rockstars. From that powerful place, you can align your message and mission, step into the spotlight, and make a powerful and positive impact on those you want to lead or serve.

A Note About the Stories You'll Read

Throughout the book, I've included stories from real people I've worked with over the years. However, in almost all instances, many details have been changed to protect their privacy—details like name, position, career focus, industry, gender, and more. If I've provided a real, full name, the story is as accurate as I can make it based on my recollections. More than once, I've had somebody say to me, when they've read an article or newsletter, "That story was about me, wasn't it?" They're never right. But that brings us to the next change I've made. In many of the stories, I've merged details from multiple stories or people to fully capture the most common struggles, opportunities, or hurdles as efficiently as possible. Because that's why I'm writing this book to begin with—to help you work through the same challenges or situations I see play out again and again and again. So, the essence of every story is true, I've tried to keep dialogue fairly close to what was actually said, and many of the changes I've made have been based on other true stories.

I don't know a single person—or team or organization—who wouldn't like to present themselves and their ideas to the world with more clarity, conviction, and passion. That's what this book offers. If you're willing to dive into the work, it will pull you out of feeling stuck, uncomfortable, unconfident. It will change the way you see yourself and the way others see you.

You'll be *believable*, and that will allow you to grow your impact and unleash possibilities in your life and work. So turn the page and get started!

PART 1

Explore Your Character

CHAPTER 2

YOUR POWER WORDS—YOUR CORE

"An actor needs a core quality or essence for a character.
Everything rises from there."[6]—Bryan Cranston

Alex was a great communicator and connecter, with his team, anyway. He was thoughtful, but also passionate, warm, and engaging. I heard that he was especially good at coaching and advocating for their career growth, and they loved him for it. All in all, Alex was a successful leader—except whenever he was forced to step into the spotlight. That roadblock was holding him back, and he knew it.

Being an advocate with the wider world was a big part of Alex's work and life. At the office, he often had to be a champion for his team when it came to decisions about budgets, resources, and support for new initiatives. Outside of work, he had launched a small nonprofit to support foster children in his community, and he needed to engage with and persuade donors, the media, and leaders of other nonprofits.

But when Alex was asked to be a compelling spokesperson for an idea or a cause in front of a group or in high-stakes situations, like when the local media had their cameras trained on him? He immediately became reserved or even hesitant, hyperfocused on data, and stiff. In other words, he was not very believable and not very persuasive. His boss told me it was hard to watch. In meetings, he wasn't gaining traction with his peers and superiors, and his team was suffering for it. With his nonprofit, the bright lights and sound bites required for fundraising pushed him out of his comfort zone, and he wasn't getting people excited about what he was trying to accomplish.

"I can feel it happening," he told me. "I know I'm not getting it right or handling these opportunities the way I want, but I can't seem to improve."

Have you ever felt this way, like you're just not nailing certain situations, especially moments that feel important? If so, you're not alone. Every person I work with has. When I asked Alex about the difference between how he showed up with his team and how he showed up in these "on stage" moments, he said, "I just feel more myself with my team."

That's an interesting phrase, *more myself*, so I asked, "What does being 'more you' mean?" That's when we hit on a big issue at the heart of Alex's believability gap. He didn't have an answer to my question.

Usually, when we're not getting a moment right, like an actor flubbing a scene onstage, or when we can tell we're not showing up consistently across the roles we play or the different situations we navigate every day, we feel like Alex did, like we aren't being ourselves. There's a gap between how we want to show up and how we actually show up—that tricky believability gap. And typically, we can sense it, but we don't fully understand it.

So I'll ask you the same question I asked Alex: Do you know who "you" is? *Because in order to* play you *compellingly and believably, you have to* know you. How can you harness the full power of who you are if you aren't sure who that is?

It's not an easy question to answer. Which may be why psychologist Tasha Eurich, author of *Insight* and self-awareness guru, has found that only 10 to 15 percent of the thousands of people she has studied are truly self-aware. And those who aren't are less effective in their roles, have less rewarding relationships, and are less trusted by others—all problems tied to believability.

Closing the believability gap has to start with a foundation of self-knowledge and insight about how you want to be in the world and how you want to show up for others. Without it, all other challenges to your believability will be a lot harder to solve. An internal believability gap can make an external believability gap wider.

Actors work hard to answer the question, "Who am I?" for every character they play. The great acting teacher Constantin Stanislavski described the fundamentals of his "method" in *An Actor Prepares* in 1936. He taught actors to use simple questions to uncover the essence of a character: What do I want? Why? What drives me? What are my strengths and challenges? Actors use questions like these to figure out where a character's power comes from and how that character will evolve and influence the story.

In this chapter I'll help you do the same for your character. To play yourself fully in the script of your own making, you have to discover how to leverage what I call your Power Words and your Power Drivers. Together, they reflect who you are fundamentally, at your core, in whatever role you're playing—what you have to offer to the world, what you value, what fuels you, and how you want to show up, day in and day out. They're an effective and efficient way to bring your amazing self into different circumstances intentionally and confidently—especially in circumstances that are new, challenging, and outside of your comfort zone. No matter what you tackle next, though, with them in hand, you'll be more confident and believable to yourself and others, growing your energy and influence.

How a Few Words Can Become the Source of Your Power in the World

"People are very specific," Oscar winner Hilary Swank once said in an interview. Everyone knows "that one thing that happened that they can't ever get out of their head, and they know their favorite color and they know the food that they don't like and they know what it is that they want to have happen…. And I find that it's super important to find specificity in characters."[7] The intensive, specific knowledge she builds has helped her connect with the innate power of each character—and earn two Oscars and lots of other awards and praise along the way. She's not alone. When we think of some of the most powerful acting in film or on stage, those who rise to the top of the list did the deep work to understand their characters deeply, fully, in specific detail, so they could portray them honestly, believably, as whole human beings.

Of course, super immersive acting can go a bit too far. When training for five hours a day as a boxer for *Million Dollar Baby*, Hilary got an infected blister on her foot and didn't tell anybody until it became life threatening. "That's what happens to boxers," she said. "They have injuries and they keep pushing through it."[8] Well, sure, but…

Extremes aside, any good actor trying to make an impact on the audience does deep research and reflection on who the character is, where they come from, what experiences shaped them, what motivates their decisions and choices. Sometimes, I want to drag the people I work with to a matinee and force them to sit in a dark theater to experience the results—to cry or laugh or feel anxious or joyful, all because of how well an actor portrays who a character is at their core, truthfully.

Why? Because regardless of their professional level—from interns to CEOs—their age, or their organization, almost all of them think that power is external, something granted by others, by a title, by a culture. But in fact, *power is impact, and it emanates from you when you truthfully convey who you are at the core, what you believe in, and what you aspire to.* I'll turn to the wisdom of Caroline McHugh, authenticity expert: "Most of us don't take up nearly the space the universe intended for us…. Which is why when you see somebody in the full flow of their humanity, it's remarkable. They're at least a foot bigger in every direction than normal human beings."[9]

Thousands of studies over decades of research have proven that greater internal self-awareness or self-knowledge boosts our power *and* our believability.

* We're better at aligning our thoughts, emotions, and goals with our words and presence (more on this in Chapter 4), which makes us more trustworthy to others.
* We make more effective personal decisions, because we have a deeper understanding of what we're trying to achieve and the values we want to live by.
* We make better career and job choices, because we understand our strengths and potential, which means a better fit, which leads to better performance and credibility.
* We're better leaders, because self-awareness often goes hand in hand with emotional intelligence.
* And overall, self-knowledge boosts our confidence and self-esteem, lowers our stress, and offers greater life satisfaction.[10]

When you can articulate who you are and what you believe and value, it's a lot easier to bring the inner you to life in the world in a way that delivers these amazing results. So in the rest of this chapter, I'll help you define your Power Words—your core defining word and your character beliefs—and your Power Drivers—your Why or purpose and your How or the mission that will help guide your behavior day to day.

Before we dive into the work, a couple of notes from your director.

Your Power Doesn't Come from Your Role or Your Results

I can't tell you how many times I've seen people try to use words like "successful" or "results-driven" or "efficient" in their Power Words. It's the epitome of the tail wagging the dog! Let's say you choose "results-driven," for instance. It can be so easy to fall victim to pre-conceptions of what that looks like in action or what other people say you need to *do* or *be* to make it happen. And that just widens the believability gap. (More on this conundrum in the next chapter and in Part 3.)

If you let other people's expectations or general circumstances guide you, you'll adopt Power Words that you don't really care about. You'll end up pulling on another ill-fitting costume, different from the one you may already be wearing. And you'll diminish the power that comes from being truthfully you. It's as former monk and bestselling author Jay Shetty wrote in *Think Like a Monk*. "Our identity is wrapped up in what others think of us—or, more accurately, what we *think* others think of us.… The 'I' and 'me,' small and vulnerable to begin with, get distorted."[11] And if we define our *selves* by our roles, when we take a hit in a role, often for reasons outside of our control, it becomes personal. It affects our sense of self, our confidence, and our inner believability.

Just remember as you go, your Power Words are the essence of *you* balanced by what's important to you, not role-dependent behaviors or outcomes. When you step into your full power, titles and hierarchy fade into the background. Your believability grows from playing you in the best possible way.

Warts and All—Kind Of

I once worked with a woman who chose *orderliness* as her core defining word. It was a less-than-ideal choice on a couple of levels, but mostly because it just wasn't true. It was an aspiration. "Do you keep your house super tidy?" I asked. "Is your life and work highly organized?" I already knew the answer based on our conversations.

"No," she said. "But I would like to."

"So why are you choosing this word as a true reflection of who you are? Just to make yourself feel bad every day?"

Too many people who take the time to do this work think of their Power Words as ideals we have to judge ourselves against. But *you can't make your Power Words a losing proposition from the start.* I understand working toward the aspirational—and that's one goal of the Power Drivers—but if you're not careful, it can just create a bigger internal believability gap.

And obviously, nobody wants to choose negative Power Words, like "boring" or "self-absorbed." And I'm not saying any of us should just because we might behave that way sometimes. But we can turn to famed acting coach Sanford Meisner for some wisdom here, who is known to have said, "To be an interesting actor—hell, to be an interesting human being—you must be authentic and for you to be authentic you must embrace who you really are, warts and all." So don't use your Power Words to try to "fix" yourself. Instead, focus on your strengths and valuable attributes and deeply held beliefs.

Because when you have given yourself the gifts of Power Words and Power Drivers that you can live by, you feel more sure of yourself and your decisions. Making choices becomes easier. You feel more comfortable in your own skin. You build deeper connections with others that help them trust you. You show up more believably day in and day out. That all combines to create a deep well of power to draw from.

Your Power Words

Your Core Defining Word

I always begin my work with people the same way:

"I want to get to know you better. Not what you do or what you know—who you *are*. So, if you could use only one word to describe who you are at the core, the essence of your being, what would that word be?"

Yes, I know this is a very reductive exercise. Every one of us can be described accurately by many words. And I'm an actor and a writer, so I love how we can layer words to build an idea or a world or a character. (My mother, who was a Freudian psychoanalyst, was the queen of describing people with so many hyperbolic words that it became a family joke. "Pamela, you are the most stupendous, outstanding, supercalifragilistic..." Eventually, we stopped believing her.) But this exercise is reductive for a reason. It helps you focus keenly on who you are. The difficulty you might have in choosing just one will help you understand the power the word can carry in your life.

Your core defining word is the foundation for your character. It's partly a reflection of who you know yourself to be and partly a reflection of how you want to show up day in and day out. *It's consistent and unchangeable.* You can't have one word for work and another for your home life—that's the opposite of what we're trying to achieve here. The goal is to be who you are, wherever you are, in all kinds of circumstances and in all parts of life.

If you're honest and thoughtful about finding your word, you'll learn so much about yourself. The words you consider and reject can be an education in how you see yourself and how you don't. Some of my favorite words that people have chosen are *ice cream*, *lighthouse*, *insight*, *banana*, and yes, the ubiquitous *passionate*. Don't be afraid of choosing what seems like a common or obvious option if it truly captures who you are! I can't tell you how many times I've been working with a group and somebody will say, "Shoot, she took my word!" Any word you choose will play out for you uniquely, based on your version, your interpretation, your definition. You'll bring it to life as only you can.

Sometimes, just taking a breath and reflecting on what you believe to be fundamentally true about yourself and what you want to offer the world can prompt the right word to show up in your mind like a shining beacon. Sometimes, though, it takes longer.

Now seems like a good time to share a deep secret. For a long time, I could not figure out my own word! Passionate? Sure. Intense? Yep. Funny? *I* think so. I'm all of these words and many others sometimes, but none of them captured how I do or want to show up in the world consistently.

My breakthrough happened when I finally listened to the great clues people were giving me. I was leading a workshop in Casablanca, Morocco, and I was told the participants expected to be entertained, to learn something, and to leave feeling connected to each other. *Suuurre*, I thought. *No problem.* But despite my nervousness, the event turned out to be a big success. As people shared their Power Words and stories that illuminated them, they laughed, they cried, but most important, they revealed things about themselves they'd never shared out loud. Even people who knew each other well were surprised by what they heard.

I was gathering my materials and getting ready for a hard-earned cocktail when a woman approached me and said, "Thank you for sharing your energy with us." I thanked her back, but in my head, I was thinking, *That's what you got out of this? C'mon...I changed some of these people's lives!*

And then it hit me. She was thanking me for bringing who *I* was at the core into that room. It was my energy that had inspired her and others to go on their own transformational journeys. And that wasn't the first time I had heard the word from friends, family, and clients. Finally, I had found my core defining word. And ever since, it has guided me and fueled me. It helped me understand what I can uniquely bring to any situation or role, and helped me discover new ways to be successful in roles I had played for years. When I focus on my energy, when I take care of myself so that I have reserves of energy, when I check my energy against my audience's needs, I'm more successful, influential, and powerful—and thus believable. The greatest compliment I've ever received was when I met a client in person for the first time after months of working together online: "Wow," she said, "your energy is exactly the same in person as it is on the screen."

Exactly. At my core, I am who I am, wherever I am and whomever I'm with.

Let's go back to Alex from the start of the chapter. To help him be more himself, so that he could be a more believable and powerful advocate, we started by working on his core defining word. Like me, he struggled. We came at it from different angles, but he kept suggesting words that reflected what others wanted him to be or what he thought he needed to be. Finally, after some work exploring why he started the nonprofit, what he loved about working with his team, and reflecting on some of his best days—when he felt effective, productive, and like he was making a real impact—his word came to him. And it surprised us both.

Father.

He was a deeply caring person who wanted to make a better world for his own children and for others. He had been influenced and inspired by his own amazing father, a Holocaust survivor. His caring persona influenced how he led his team, the kind of brave advocate he could be for them in key moments and that he knew he could be more consistently with the right focus.

When he finally overcame the business-speak cliches and chose a word that initially he would have said was too "soft," the shift was amazing. He connected his role as an advocate to his heartfelt desire to help his company and team grow. He pulled back from relying on data and outcomes and spoke more passionately about ideas and initiatives. He found a way to be more himself in communicating about the nonprofit. And he became so much more persuasive, inspiring, and effective!

Two Rules and One Non-Rule

Now it's your turn. But first, I want to share my two rules and one non-rule for the word you choose.

- ★ Rule 1: It can't be situational—late, tired, hungry—or role dependent (I've explained what a bad idea that is).
- ★ Rule 2: Consider what your friends and family and possibly colleagues would say about it. There's always at least one guy who chooses the word *inspirational,* for instance, and everyone else is thinking, *Uh…nope.* Standing in the front of the room, I can see the smirks and shaking heads behind him. Most of us have some blind spots about who we are and how we show up, both positive and less than positive. *The key is to not be controlled by the perceptions of others but also be aware that you might find some good clues there,* like I did.
- ★ Non-rule 3: You can consider or choose any type of word you like—a noun, an adjective, a verb, anything except an acronym because that's cheating. If you're getting stuck on the type of word, think about some of your favorite words and use them as a starting point.

Once you decide on a word, you might have to live with it for a while before completely committing to it. Of course, that requires you to be conscious and aware of how your behavior is connected to it in different circumstances—and that's important work no matter what, work that we'll get into in the rest of the book.

Your Core Defining Word

1. Find a quiet place to think, take a breath, and consider what makes you wonderfully unique and of value to the people you impact. Try thinking back to your last few really great days. Everything is working—your relationships, your accomplishments, how you handled sticky situations. How you showed up felt easy or natural, not forced. What word would you use to describe you on those days?

2. Make a short list of words that come to mind.

   - Remember the two rules for the words you consider seriously. (1) They can't be situational or role dependent. (2) You have to consider what your friends and family would say about the word.

   - If you're not sure about a word, take a moment to imagine yourself in different situations in your life, especially in challenging situations where you might be operating outside your comfort zone. What would it mean to show up in those situations as this word? Is that truly how you *want* to show up in the world, or how you think you can bring the essence of who you are to life?

   - Could others tell stories about you and use that word as the theme?

   - Does the word you're considering inspire you to take hope-filled action in a positive way? Does it energize you and make you smile and feel good?

3. If your word is not coming to you, release yourself and come back to it later. I can attest that just by thinking about it, you'll begin the process of believing in your own unique strength and value. And eventually your word will appear.

Your Character Beliefs

Every decision we make, every sentence we say, is guided on some level by what I call our character beliefs—what's most important to us or our values. They shape our thinking when we're making decisions or developing views about ourselves, other people, or the world. Our core defining word might be a point of focus for how we show up in the world, but our character beliefs create a guidance system that influences how we think and behave. They help us align big and small decisions and behaviors with who we are at our core.

What's always surprising to me is how often people can rattle off their company's values, but not their own. I once asked a group of 300 CEOs how many had defined their company values. Every single one raised a hand. "Great. Now, how many of you have done it for yourself?" Three of them raised a hand. Yup. Three.

And then something powerful happened. One of the three called out and asked for the microphone. "I want to tell you why I was forced to identify my character beliefs," he said. "One day, years ago, all of my employees quit." He had founded a company and grown it to dozens of employees—and every one of them had walked out.

As he scrambled to recover and try to convince people to come back, he learned some hard truths. Let's face it, people don't quit en masse for great, self-aware leaders. He was *really* hard to work for. He didn't treat people well. He was demanding. And they had no idea what they were working toward. People didn't trust him and they clearly didn't believe in him.

It was a rough call to action. But what action? He realized he wasn't sure. He couldn't articulate why he was building the company, why the work mattered to him, what kind of leader he wanted to be. He needed a guidance system, so he dug in and figured it out. And his defined values changed how he showed up for his team, where he decided to take his business next, and a million other decisions and behaviors.

How can well-defined character beliefs help you be more believable? Well, your decisions become more consistent and predictable to the people around you. It's much easier to act in alignment with your beliefs and course correct if you aren't, before the believability gap grows too wide. All of that lessens the internal conflict that rises out of making choices or acting in opposition to our values, which is a big cause of stress. When we act in alignment with them, we feel happier and more satisfied. As Mark Manson, author of *The Subtle Art of Not Giving a F*ck*, wrote, "Personal values are the measuring sticks by which we determine what is a successful and meaningful life."[12] When we understand what "meaningful" looks like to us, we're more likely to achieve it. And of course, nobody chooses bad values, so when you rely on them, you show up as your best self more often.

Our character beliefs can drive our behavior in the moments that matter most, which is why as an actor, it's not nearly enough to know what I'm supposed to say or do. I have to understand *why* I'm saying and doing those things to bring the character to life truthfully.

How do you do this when you don't have a script to turn to for insights? You can start with a list—there are plenty online—but one note of caution. Remember that you are being thoughtful about what is important to *you* and what you want to guide *your* behavior. Don't let the words on a list override what you probably already know to be true about yourself, on some level. Which is why I recommend looking inside first by thinking deeply about the series of questions that I've shared at the end of this section and then use a list to find words that best capture those truths. Most people discover that, with a bit of reflection, some values rise to the top and feel immutable.

As you work on your character beliefs, focus on refining your list to just three. I'm not saying that's all that might be important to you, but it's not easy to remember, focus on, or balance more than a handful of ideas as we navigate the many, many decisions we make every day. You'll give yourself a clearer guide if you focus on those that are most important to you. You can always adjust as you try to apply them in the real world. For a long time, one of my character beliefs was *family*. But while I love them, they can cause me a lot of angst. I realized that as a value, "family" can be fraught. I spent some time contemplating what felt good to me or was important to me about family, and I realized it was all about having deep connections and showing up for people with love and respect. *Connectedness* is what I truly value.

No matter what beliefs you choose, once you have them in mind, you'll be able to leverage them to grow your impact on the world.

Identifying Your Character Beliefs

While we can see our values show up in small moments—in all moments, really—sometimes they're easier to spot in big moments. Think about some of the most inspiring and meaningful moments of your life or a great accomplishment. Even if we're not fully conscious of or intentional about it, what guides us to and through those kinds of moments is often what's most important to us—our deepest character beliefs.

Thinking about these moments, reflect on the following questions and write down the words that best capture what you believe or value, not what you do well or specific actions you've taken.

- What kind of priorities guided you in your meaningful moments?

- What kinds of behaviors helped you achieve big successes?

- What about those moments make you feel proud, like you did the right thing for yourself and for others?

- What thinking or behaviors helped you overcome problems or navigate difficult decisions or situations?

- What words describe how you worked with others or how you sustained important relationships along the way?

Finally, as you consider your answers or the words you've written down, answer this overarching question: What few values shine through that you want to guide you in all parts of your life?

Your Power Drivers

Your Why

Tula was an actuary—you know, the people who look at death tables all day. You may have even heard the joke, "Actuaries are people who are too boring to be accountants." I don't think that's true at all, but Tula was self-aware enough to know that was how she was perceived by others. (I was actually very excited to work with an actuary because I had played one on TV! Well, in a training video for the American Academy of Actuaries.)

As we dove into our work together, though, I found Tula to be an extremely thoughtful, emotional, and generous soul. She understood that her work made possible the financial futures of the company's clients and their families. Her role as an actuary wasn't about death at all, but about legacy. Impact, not endings. And *impact* became her core defining word.

I wanted to help her turn that word into an inspiring guide, to capture her Why, her purpose, in a way that turned her core defining word into a powerful journey. As psychologist Mihaly

Csikszentmihalyi, who explored and explained the "flow" state of optimal experience, once told Dan Pink, who interviewed him for the book *Drive*, "Purpose provides activation energy for living."[13] And Dan Pink identified it as one of the three essential ingredients of motivation (along with autonomy and mastery). I sometimes even use the term character motivation because that's what finding our purpose—our Why—gives us. Think of an actor asking, "What's my character's motivation?" What they're really asking is what's my character's objective, their higher level purpose, the driving force behind their choices and behaviors in the story or scene.

Psychologists have found that a strong purpose has three components: It gives you something to strive for. It's personally meaningful. And it reflects the contribution you want to make to others.[14] So having a defined purpose gives you the double motivation of going on a journey toward something that matters to you and that matters to the world. And being committed to a clear purpose can make you more resilient in the face of adversity. You're quicker to positively reframe negative events.[15] It levels up your grit and perseverance.[16] All of this boosts your believability by revealing the positive impact you want to have and by allowing you to show up more consistently as your best self.

So it may be obvious why I believe your purpose should be aligned with the essence of who you are at your core and what you offer the world.

I'll admit, though, that it can be hard to answer the big question, "What's my motivation for my life?" or "Why do I exist?" early on in this kind of work. I often tell clients that we'll come back to it as we tackle other elements of bringing who we are to the world. It's more important that you pick your Power Words and craft the easier How statement that brings your character beliefs into focus and can be a simple guide for your behavior. But articulating a Why statement is still important to your believability to align who you are at your core with an articulated purpose. Knowing it can create an incredibly strong foundation for believing in yourself.

Tula's Why finally revealed itself when she was asked to chair a gala for the local diabetes treatment center, where she had lost her beloved sister a few years before. As we worked on her speech, she realized she had learned a powerful lesson from her sister—make the world a better place. She shared her sister's impact in her speech, including her new Why statement: To use my talents and abilities to make a positive impact on the world. Her Why gave her a new kind of purposeful presence. She no longer leads with "boring actuary" when people ask what she does or who she is. She's someone who is making a positive impact, and that's not boring at all.

Your Why Statement

Again, take focused time out of your day to reflect. Think of a time when you embodied your core defining word. How did the word guide your behavior or energize you? Next, think into the future.

- How would you like to bring your core defining word to life going forward?

- What meaningful aspiration would you like to achieve through it, over the long term?

- What impact would you like to make on others or your community by leveraging it?

Now, write a simple, one-sentence statement that motivates you, that makes your word soar for you, and that boosts your internal and external believability.

Your How

Your character beliefs are just words unless you use them to guide your behavior and communication. And that's where the How statement comes in. *How* are you going to bring your values to life daily? *How* will you play you? Without a How statement, it will be hard to actually live by your values or pay attention to them consistently, especially in difficult moments. Your How becomes a kind of affirmation of who you are and what you're trying to achieve day in and day out. And research has shown that these kinds of value-driven affirmations calm the threat response center of the brain, reducing our stress and anxiety in the face of difficult circumstances.[17]

It doesn't have to be complicated. In fact, it shouldn't be. *You can't pay attention to complicated.* Your guide for how you want to show up and how you want to be perceived should be simple, clear, and actionable. If it's got too many words or any semicolons, if it doesn't come trippingly off the tongue, you'll never actually pay attention to it.

It also can, and probably should be, role dependent. It's okay to translate your character beliefs into behaviors in slightly different ways depending on what role you're playing in the moment. It's okay for this guide to look a little different for how you're showing up at work and outside of work. I've seen people develop How statements for their role at work, for their important relationships, for how they want to show up as a parent.

My How statement for the work I do is, "I help others present themselves and their stories with passion through humor, excellence, and deep connectedness." It is a positive representation of who I am in the world of my work. And it helps me think about how I can use my character beliefs to impact others. Here are some other good examples:

★ "I am a detail-oriented and organized leader who fosters joy and empowers growth."

* ★ "I'm a fun-loving creative who delivers high-quality work by holding myself and others accountable."
* ★ "I'm a trusted partner who prioritizes my clients' success by delivering with excellence and consistency."

Now it's your turn.

Crafting Your How

You can give yourself a starting point by thinking of your How statement like a personal Mad Libs. Use the fill-in sentence below and add in a word that describes the fundamentals of your role (like leader, creative, partner from above), your three character beliefs, and what you're ultimately trying to accomplish day to day.

I am a _______ who believes in _______, _______, and _______ in order to _______.

Then revise it into a simple sentence that helps you focus on how you want to bring your values to life in your role, like the examples I've shared.

Use What You've Discovered as a Daily Guide

You've done some amazing work on the foundation for your believability, on exploring the core of your character—who you are, what's important to you, and how you want to be in the world. Now you have to give life to these ideas, to set them as your guidance system and pay attention to how you are living them.

I'll share what I always suggest to my clients: Start by turning them into *"My power on a Post-it note."* Write your Power Words (core defining words plus your character beliefs) on a couple of Post-its. Do the same for your Power Drivers (Why plus How statements). Put the Post-its in a couple of spots where you can easily see them and let them guide your "every days." Throughout the day, check in with them. Are you bringing them to life in your role? Are others seeing them in your choices, your behavior, your communication?

I love when my clients share pictures of their Post-it notes and stories about how seeing them has guided their behavior in meaningful moments. I can't wait for you to craft and post yours—and discover that by doing so you are one big step closer to bridging your internal believability gap.

CHAPTER 3

CLUES IN THE SCRIPT—YOUR ROLE

"It's the character you bring to your role as an
actor and human being…which is and will
always be simply you."[18]—BARRY BOSTWICK

"You're taking me and my whole team away from a day of important work to 'get to know each other better.'" I could hear the air quotes in Rebecca's tone. I knew she could be direct, no-nonsense, so her skeptical answer to my question about what her team could get out of the program we were planning didn't exactly surprise me. But it also explained why her boss had brought me in to begin with. The team wasn't gelling, he had said, and their collaboration and creativity weren't hitting the mark. That's usually a sign that people aren't comfortable bringing their whole, truthful selves to their roles. And that kind of problem often starts at the top.

"I'd like to learn more about you so that I can understand why you might feel that way."

I *was* a little surprised when Rebecca dove right in, telling me about her childhood, which wasn't overflowing with opportunity, how she put herself through college, and how hard she worked to make it in the male-dominated manufacturing industry. As we turned to the topic of her leadership approach, she said something that shocked me into silence—which for me is a *big* deal. "I have to remind myself to say thank you to the people on my team," she said. "I think their paycheck is a thank you, and I don't really understand this need for constant appreciation."

Eventually, I recovered from my fainting spell and said, "I think that's something we need to unpack with your people."

"I would never say that to them!"

"Maybe not in those words, but I'm here to help you find a safe way to talk to them about what you hope to achieve *and their expectations for how you play your role.*" Because based on her performance reviews and the team atmosphere, their expectations were definitely not being met. "And then you can find opportunities to meet their expectations by being more of who you are, at your core."

In the last chapter, I explained that your power doesn't come from your role or results, it comes from who you are at your core, what is important to you, and what drives you—all elements of your character. *However, your potential power doesn't become real impact until you learn how to bring your character to life within the circumstances of the role you're playing.*

You are not living in a one-person improv show, perpetually playing you alone in an empty theater. Your role is one part—a necessary and important part—in a "production" of a story. That story includes

- ★ Other players who are trying to succeed in their roles— your bosses, direct reports, your partner, your kids
- ★ Specific plot points that require your unique talents and skills to drive the story forward
- ★ A setting or culture that influences everybody

Understanding the nuances of Why and how a particular role makes an impact is one thing great actors do well, because it helps them bring the full power of their character to the needs of each scene to increase the impact. So whenever I was cast in a new role, once I was familiar with who my character was at their core, I would go deeper into the script, mining it for clues that revealed how my character needed to behave to contribute at a high level to the story and support the other players.

The same is true for you. To play you believably in a given role, you can leverage the core strengths and unique qualities of your character to meet the demands of the circumstances and the needs and expectations of other players. The more you bring your core character to the role, the more powerfully you'll play it, and the more energy and progress you can generate in the collective story. You'll feel more confident, you'll make more progress, you'll contribute more to your team and culture, and you'll close the believability gap.

Unfortunately, most of us struggle with this. We hold back our true character instead of bringing that character to life, showing up as a shadow of our whole selves. Adam Grant wrote powerfully about this struggle in *Originals*. "Although America is a land of individuality and unique self-expression, in search of excellence and in fear of failure, most of us opt to fit in rather than stand out.... We find surface ways of appearing original—donning a bow tie, wearing bright red shoes—without taking the risk of actually being original. When it comes to the powerful ideas in our heads and the core values in our hearts, we censor ourselves."[19]

When it comes to a given role, we're too focused on how we're *supposed* to play it or how we *want* to play it or how well others are playing *their* roles. We miss clues about how well we're responding to others' needs, how often we're delivering our best, or whether we're showing up as we want to in our environment. Sometimes, we get obvious clues, flashing bright and right in front of us, like a rave review or a negative review, like a big promotion or a blowup with a colleague. But usually, the clues about how we could bring more of our unique, believable self to a role are more subtle and we don't make the effort to hunt for them.

Take Rebecca, who didn't see the value in recognition. Of *course* we discovered that she had a serious believability gap with her team. When we were all together, I could tell they were hesitant to share their thoughts, because she seemed distant and impatient—at least at first. When she did express appreciation, it seemed insincere. They didn't believe she cared about what they had to say or how they felt. They all had expectations that weren't being met of what their leader would bring to the team. Like most of us, they wanted to be empowered, inspired, and encouraged. But Rebecca wasn't even offering basic appreciation or recognition. The culture Rebecca was feeding through her behavior was bringing everybody's performance down and making it harder for Rebecca to be successful in her role.

"You are not *you* in a vacuum," I told her after our day with the team. "You are *you* with and for the people you wish to impact, lead, or serve—all the other characters in the story you're trying to create."

You can't hide who you are at your core and expect to receive rave reviews in your role. And you can't use your authenticity like a bludgeon, either. That's kind of what Rebecca was doing. An "I'm gonna be me and everybody else can just deal with it" mindset isn't any more effective than an "I'm gonna be who they want me to be and then they'll like and respect me" mindset. *The key is to find the powerful middle ground by understanding what you uniquely bring to a role and how you can truthfully meet the needs of the circumstances and fulfill the expectations of others.* Then you'll be able to respond and react in ways that are genuine, generous, and that build connection and belief.

Have you found that powerful middle ground in your role? Do you understand the story you're contributing to? Do you know how to contribute in a way that supports your fellow players? Have you considered what you have to bring to the role, just by being uniquely you? Remember, no matter what words they're expected to say, what actions they're expected to perform, *great actors make the role their own, and you can too.* I saw Ian McKellen, who famously played Gandalf in *The Lord of the Rings*, play the evil Iago in *Othello*. Christopher Walken played the same character in a Shakespeare in the Park production in Central Park. You can bet that both actors were amazing, fulfilling every demand and expectation of the role, but in dramatically different and wonderfully unique ways.

That's the power *you* have in any role when you bring your true character to it. So let's start looking for clues that reveal your greatest opportunities to bring your character to life and be more effective, inspiring, and successful.

Where to Find Important Clues for Bringing Yourself to Your Role

Like a lot of actors, I use a few strategies as I search for insights about my role in the script. First, I draw on Constantin Stanislavski's methods and ask questions like, "How does my character's behavior support or undermine the progress of the story? What do other characters say about my character? What does that say about their expectations, and what can I bring to the role to enhance how my character meets or defies those expectations?" Then I review the stage directions. In a few short words, they can capture a whole lot of information, especially how a character interacts with others and the expectations of the director and the other actors on the stage with me—where will I be and what will I be doing?

Wouldn't it be great, at least sometimes, to be handed a literal script for the role you're playing, a guide to tell you exactly how to respond or behave when you're unsure of yourself? Something to explain the nuances of the story playing out all around you, or how and when to hit your mark? Just because you don't have that kind of script, with precise stage movements and dialogue, doesn't mean you aren't inundated with information and clues. In your professional role especially, you have a lot of material to work with:

- ★ Performance reviews and comments from your boss in one-on-one meetings
- ★ Your job description

★ Things your boss has said about how they want the team to function or what kind of culture they're trying to create

★ Official company values and mission and purpose statements

★ Things company leaders have said about company priorities and culture development

★ If you're a leader, employee engagement surveys might indicate how well you're meeting the needs and expectations of the people on your team

Put all of this together and you've got a wealth of information about expectations for your role, how your role contributes to the success or growth of the team and company, what skills, talents, and behaviors can help you succeed, and the circumstances or culture that create the backdrop. That tells you a lot about the story you're contributing to.

But I'll be honest. This is the point at which a lot of people run into a brick wall, because I ask them to look for clues in feedback they've received. It can be easy to interpret the clues as attacks and get defensive, to see them as signs of failure and become self-critical, or to see them as more important than our own knowledge of what we have to offer. Essentially, we can interpret them as proof that who we are isn't enough or that we can't bring our whole selves to the role—rather than finding opportunities to do the opposite! The question we should ask about feedback is this, "Is this a clue that I am or am not showing up as me in my role?"

Let's go back to Rebecca. You might be thinking, *She's a jerk and if that's her being her truthful self, she should try to hide it as much as possible.* In fact, she's not a jerk. She just didn't understand how to bring her character beliefs and her How statement to life to accomplish her goals *in a way that aligns with others' needs and the expectations of the role.* She was missing the clues. She had chosen *dedicated* as her core defining word and her character beliefs were accountability, curiosity, and perseverance. They all rang true to me. I had given her the assignment to develop a How statement and she had come up with, *I'm a curious and accountable leader who helps my team persevere through challenges to deliver powerful results.*

Her performance review had a fair amount to say about how great she was at responding to requests from other teams, at delivering work on time, at getting things accomplished—all signs of dedication and accountability. And it had a fair amount to say about her leadership approach, as interpreted by her team, and how it was affecting their creative collaboration. Work was being delivered competently, but the team wasn't necessarily delivering powerful results.

"I know you're an avid learner, but with your team, are you being curious?" I asked. "And I know you're great at holding yourself accountable to meeting the demands of other departments and leaders, but are you holding yourself accountable to meeting the needs of your team? Because that's what it takes to be the kind of leader you say you want to be."

It was an eye-opening moment for Rebecca, seeing how she was living her values somewhat selectively. The fact that her team didn't see them in her behavior as she was playing her role was a big cause of her believability gap.

Based on the work you did in the previous chapter, I want you to look for clues about how and where you're bringing your character to life and successfully meeting the needs and expectations of your role—and where you have opportunities to grow. You can use the next exercise to do the same kind of insight-generating work Rebecca did. Then the rest of the chapter will help you explore opportunities for bringing more of yourself to your role and your culture.

Clues About Whether You're Bringing Your Character to Life in Your Role

Gather any feedback you can. Formal performance reviews are a good place to start, especially 360 reviews. If you have one-on-ones with your boss, consider what you've discussed about how to improve or grow. Consider anything you've heard or read from your colleagues and teammates. When have they thanked you or praised you and what specifics did they mention? When have they asked for you to show up or contribute differently?

As you answer the following questions, keep your Power Words and Power Drivers handy to remind yourself what you want to bring to your role, what you're trying to achieve in it, and how you want to play it based on your unique character.

- What clues do you see about where and how you're successfully bringing your true self to your role?

- What clues do you see that you're *not* showing up as you want to, that people aren't seeing your true character?

- What clues do you see that you're successfully meeting others' expectations of and the demands of the role?

- What clues do you see that you're not?

Make notes about what you discover—where you're succeeding and where you have opportunities to bring more of yourself to the role to be more successful. Then, with these valuable clues in hand, work through the rest of the exercises in this chapter.

Turn Your Job Description
into a *Role* Description

Recently, researchers from the London School of Economics and University of Chicago ran an interesting study. Working in one large company, they took a group of 3,000 employees and had them participate in a workshop. In the workshop, they did exercises very much like those I shared in the last chapter and this chapter—reflecting on important moments in their lives, defining their character beliefs, articulating their Why, and reflecting on how all of that aligned with their current roles. As they followed the participants over time, they found that while some people left their roles because they discovered a misalignment, the people who stayed performed better in their roles.[20]

Understanding who we are at our core and how that aligns with our role helps us bring our strengths, values, and mission to life, which makes us more successful. You probably know this inherently, and I've seen the idea in action through my work, which is why I crafted the next exercise. And it was an important part of the work I did with Rebecca.

A How statement is a starting point for how you want to play you and bring your character beliefs to life in your role, but it can be important to go deeper and get more specific about what that looks like day to day, while fulfilling all of the responsibilities of a role in ever-changing circumstances.

For Rebecca, we specifically needed to find ways to connect her character to the bigger, important role of leader, beyond the tasks and deliverables of being a department head, which were the focus of her *job* description. We used her character beliefs and How statement to capture how she could lead her team to new heights, meeting their needs while delivering the excellent, collaborative work the company needed from them. We aligned how she wanted to show up, the demands of the role, and the expectations of others into a document that she could turn to for guidance and daily self-coaching. And it made a substantial difference.

That's the power of a role description.

I've written the next exercise with a focus on your professional role, but you could adapt it for just about any role you play in life.

Write Your Role Description

A role description isn't the same as a job description. It goes beyond tasks and expectations to capture how you can succeed and add value by paying attention to your Power Words and Power Drivers, especially your How.

- Get a current copy of your job description. If what's available doesn't match what you do anymore, ask your boss to update it before doing this exercise.

- Spend some time writing about what is expected of you, beyond what's outlined in the job description, which may be high level and only really capture half or two-thirds of what you spend your time doing, day in and day out.

- With those elements in hand, turn your attention to your Power Words and Power Drivers. Reread your How statement and start thinking about opportunities to bring it to life by turning it into specific behaviors important to your role.

- Now, write a personalized role description. It should reflect the requirements and expectations and how your unique character qualifies you to fulfill them—and add even more value. Weave your core defining word, character beliefs, and How statement through, as you think about how you can be most successful and satisfied in the role.

What if You're Still Feeling Miscast?

My very first paid acting role—one that earned me a whopping ten-dollar check that I still have today—was as a dominatrix. Yep. I was committing every sexual harassment infraction set out by the Equal Employment Opportunity Commission (EEOC) on a man on stage, teaching him a lesson after he had done the same to a woman in his office. Now, I'm not saying I'm a prude, but there's a long, winding road between that label and "dominatrix." I was supposed to play the role with abandon, but I really struggled to let go. I was so uncomfortable, I couldn't bring a truthful character to it, and the director was pretty frustrated with me. I was not doing a very good job of closing the believability gap for the audience.

I did get *one* awkward compliment from my partner in the vignette, Brian. One night, my husband, came to the play and Brian and I were chatting with him afterward. Suddenly, Brian said to my husband, "Well, you must be impressive."

"Why?" my husband asked, confused.

"Well, you know she has to grab me by the crotch at one point. I put three tube socks in my pants and she didn't even blink."

I turned bright red.

A common question I get when people do the exercises I've already described is, "What if I discover that I *have* been miscast?" What if there's a massive gap between who you are and the big and small expectations of your role? Then, like some of the people in the study I described in the previous section, it may be time to look for a new opportunity that closes that gap a bit for you. But in any role you're playing right now, it's unlikely that you've been seriously miscast, like I was as a dominatrix. If you feel generally satisfied by your work and are often successful in it, you probably haven't been miscast at all. And yet, you might still feel uncomfortable in your role at times.

It may be the stress of dealing with people higher up the ladder. "My boss doesn't get me," I often hear. Or worse, "My boss doesn't care what I have to offer." True, some leaders aren't great at making people feel connected or valued for their unique contributions, usually because they haven't been taught how. Sometimes, though, it's our own internal scripts making us feel we can't be ourselves with "higher-ups." Again, we'll dig into uncovering and rewriting those scripts in Part 3.

Sometimes, it's not about feeling miscast from the start but finding ourselves becoming uncomfortable or uninspired in a role over time. Roles evolve, companies change, bosses change, teams change, new tasks get layered on, and we can lose clarity and connection with our Why and How. *We struggle to answer the question, "Why am I here? Why am I uniquely qualified to shine in this role?"*

Anika, a human resources leader who had been hired to help a lean, mean, entrepreneurial company as it grew, was facing this exact challenge. The CEO's vision was to grow to 300 employees fast, and that's where he expected Anika to contribute. Her seven page job description highlighted her human resources responsibilities, but during the hiring process he made it clear he needed somebody who could develop a vision for talent growth and culture development.

As time went on, though, all of that exciting work was crowded out by the minutia of payroll, recruiting, and writing job descriptions. The leadership team felt frustrated that she wasn't living up to their expectations, and they started treating her like an order taker rather than a visionary. The consequences of Anika's unhappiness were showing up in her responsiveness and even thoroughness—a real problem when you're dealing with payroll! Her believability gap was widening every day, internally and externally.

Of course, we started by defining her Power Words and Power Drivers, something I did with the whole executive team. In my one-on-one work with Anika, she was frank about feeling miscast, especially when it came to her character beliefs of innovation, personal growth, and inclusion, and her core defining word of "inspiring." "I don't see how I can bring this all to life in this role. Not with everything they've put on my plate."

I could see the disconnect, and how her believability was taking a hit because she was mired in tasks, rather than proactively offering solutions for building engagement, growing the culture, and helping the company realize its vision. "To me, it's clear that you can be successful in this role and that what the CEO wants is somebody with your values. However, I think it's time to have a courageous conversation with him," I told her.

If you feel like somebody who is trying to fit into a role that's too far from who you fundamentally are, it's time to have a conversation with your director. That's what an actor would do. They would ask, "Why did you cast me in this role? What did you see in me? What about my past work made you think I could bring something unique or interesting to this role? What was the spark?" I was such a newbie actor when I played the dominatrix, I didn't take those steps and it hurt my performance. The important flip side of having this kind of conversation is that it's an opportunity to align expectations about role responsibilities with what you have to offer. It can be an important reminder for your director that expands your believability with them.

Because of my own experience, I knew that's where Anika needed to begin, even before working on her role description. She already had clues about what wasn't working. She needed insights about why others thought she could shine in the role, and she needed to remind them of those attributes of her character that could help her contribute to the company's progress. She set a meeting with the CEO and asked the kinds of questions I've shared in the next exercise. Each spawned an important conversation in which they both were able to reorient their thinking about the role and what it required. The CEO acknowledged that they had hired her believing that she could "do it all," but that in reality, if what they really wanted was a growth-oriented visionary, they needed to find a way to free her up. And that allowed her to be future-oriented in the moment.

"If our plan is to get to 200 employees by the end of next year," she said, "we need to consider building out the HR function to support that now. We either need to outsource some of this or we need to bring on at least one more person to handle more of the operational components."

You can initiate a conversation with your "director" at any time to remind yourself and them why *you* specifically are in this role, which can boost the confidence you need to be more intentionally *you* in it—and align their expectations with the unique value you can bring to it.

A Conversation with Your Director

Set a meeting with your manager, boss, mentor, the person who cast you in your role, or the person who urged you to go for the role. Let them know you want to understand better what they think you do or can bring to it. Try asking the following questions to get to meaty insights and feedback.

- What did you see in me?

- What was the skill set you thought would help me be successful?

- What does this role need that you thought I was uniquely qualified to offer?

- Do you think the role or the needs of the role have changed?

- Where do you think I could bring more of my talents to the role?

Tackling the Elusive "Culture Fit"

Nick was a hang glider—a pretty dangerous sport that's definitely not for the faint of heart. We were working on his Power Words when he told me about this passion. We were trying to pin down his character beliefs and I had asked him what was important to him outside of work. As I probed for more information about what to me seemed like the kind of thing an mad person with a death wish might choose to do, something important came to light.

"Risk-taking is really important to you," I said.

"I can't choose that!" he said.

See, Nick worked on a team of trustees for a large family charitable trust. He was a trusted advisor responsible for billions of dollars invested on other people's behalf. "The financial futures of these small nonprofits depend on the choices I make," he explained. "And so does the legacy of this family. I mean, just look around this place." I immediately understood what he meant.

The offices were full of dark paneling, hushed conversations, lots of people silently analyzing the market. Everybody wore a suit and some donned the serious third piece—the power vest. The company's values included integrity, excellence, and knowledge. This was not a rowdy Masters of the Universe kind of crowd. If I were writing a script with the scene line, "Interior: a hyper-conservative financial firm," this is what I would be imagining.

Even though Nick spent his days managing financial risk, he felt the culture was really about mitigating it so that they never lost their clients' money. Despite the fact that his track record was impeccable, he felt that to say that one of his character beliefs was risk-taking would put him at odds with the culture. And the core defining word that he kept coming back to and then shying away from? *Adventure*. Ooh…dangerous.

"Nick, you are not the culture of this organization," I told him. "You play a role within it. And how you interpret your Power Words within the context of this culture is everything. If I was picking somebody to grow my wealth, I'd want the guy who knows how to leap off a cliff and land safely, still alive. Being a successful risk-taker means approaching high-stakes situations with careful consideration of all the possibilities so that you can adjust in the moment. And somebody who chooses *adventure* as their core defining word is somebody who is curious, who wants to learn and explore. These are all qualities I'd want on my financial team. And they're all qualities that are expected in your role."

I can't tell you how often I hear from clients, "You don't understand the culture here" or "I can't be authentic here. It wouldn't work." I know there are situations where that might be true, but I think it's rarer than we might think. However, it doesn't change how we respond when we feel that way. Let's look first at the common behavior of covering, and then we'll turn to an exercise to help you discover all of the ways you align with and can bring more of your character to your culture. It might require a little courage, but that's how we can each influence the cultures we play our roles within, for the better.

The Problem of Covering

When Ben Kingsley began his acting career, his given name was Krishna Pandit Banji. He changed it because "he understood that it could be career consequential for him to present himself as his full authentic self," explained Kenji Yoshino, director of the Meltzer Center for Diversity, Inclusion, and Belonging at New York University, professor of constitutional law, and expert on covering.[21] That's what Ben Kingsley was doing, toning down aspects of his identity to blend into the mainstream culture of his industry, beginning with his name. And yet, he earned his first Oscar when he was cast in a role that required him to be more of his whole authentic self—Gandhi.

It's easy to say, "be you!" in a role. It's a lot harder to do it, especially when you feel that *you* are fundamentally different from the mainstream culture or cultural expectations of the role you're in. It's true for all of us to some degree, which is why covering is a rampant behavior. It's more true for people who have been historically marginalized. (Code-switching and masking are similar.) They feel uncomfortable precisely because of subtle and overt messages that, given who they are—their gender or gender identity, their race or ethnicity, their sexual identity, their socioeconomic background, and a host of other "otherness"—they aren't the right person for their role or their organization. If you're told that you've been miscast just by being you, of course you're going to hide aspects of your identity to sidestep discrimination.

I saw the behavior in Rebecca from the start of the chapter. She wasn't transparent with her team or her peers about her background because many of the other leaders at her level had MBAs from top-tier schools. It had taken her six years to finish college, because she had to work almost full time, and she got her MBA in her later thirties through a local night school program. As a woman in the manufacturing industry, she had had to push hard to get ahead, but I learned quickly that she didn't like to talk about any of that.

Deloitte has done extensive research on the problem of covering at work and found that 70 percent of disabled people do it, 69 percent of nonheterosexual people do it, and 62 to 66 percent of women and Black, Asian, or Hispanic people do it.[22] Regardless of why we cover, it leads to stress, anxiety, and other big negative effects:

- ★ 60 percent of people who participated in the survey said covering hurt their overall well-being and left them "feeling emotionally drained."
- ★ 58 percent said it damaged their sense of self.
- ★ 54 percent said it hurt their ability to do their job to the best of their ability.

Covering pulls us away from our greatest source of power and impact—our uniqueness. That was true for Rebecca. Her background made her the hard worker she was, and it helped give context to her expectations for her team.

Working to bridge the believability gap can't solve systemic discrimination or fix every crappy culture in the world that makes people feel they have to cover, but I do believe it will make a dent in that second problem. In the wise words of Brené Brown, "True belonging only happens when we present our authentic, imperfect selves to the world."[23] *Building the habits of believability can encourage you to bring more of your whole self to your role on your terms, in a way that reduces your sense of risk.*

What you need, and what Nick and Rebecca both needed, to strike the right balance are clues about how to shine, uniquely and truthfully, in your role.

Looking for Similarities, Not Differences

It helps to understand how you and the culture overlap, so in a moment, I'm going to have you do that valuable analysis. But two points of caution first.

★ The goal isn't to change who you are to fit in. The goal is to understand how who you are at the core of your character overlaps with defining characteristics of the culture(s) you operate in as you fulfill your role.

★ It can be easy to be distracted by the differences, especially if you're feeling that you don't quite fit in. Your human cognitive bias can lead you to focus on the negative: "I'm a free spirit and this place is so conservative." It's important to try to put that mindset aside and focus on commonalities—how you can positively contribute, not how you are fundamentally different.

By talking through this kind of analysis, Nick was able to see opportunities to be more open about who he is, to talk about his character beliefs, and to genuinely contribute to the culture in meaningful ways. And it made him more believable because people sensed a commitment from him to have a positive impact, a higher level of engagement, that hadn't been there before. Rebecca was able to do the same, by better understanding how she could leverage her own character beliefs to improve the culture of the team that she was so heavily influencing.

You can find that power, too. Start with the exercise I've shared here and see what insights it offers.

The Intersection of You and the Culture

Do this exercise for both your team culture and your company culture. They should be similar, but they often won't be identical.

1. Take a piece of paper and draw a line down the center of it, about two-thirds of the way down. Then draw a line across the page, like an upside down T, creating a separate section at the bottom.

2. On one side, write your Power Words and your Power Drivers.

3. On the other side, write anything you know about the culture, especially anything that's been communicated formally or informally. For instance, your company's official values and mission statement, what your boss has said about the kind of team environment they want to create, and even what you've heard people say about the culture that rings true to you.

> 4. Take some time to consider behaviors that support both your Power Words and Power Drivers and attributes of the culture you've written down. Let's say "excellence" is your core defining word and "integrity" is a company value. How does your interpretation of excellence support and amplify integrity in the company?
>
> 5. At the bottom of the page, write down what you discover as you look for overlap, supporting behaviors, and how bringing more of your whole self to your role enhances the culture and can help you feel more part of it.

Every one of us—all the performers on the stage, no matter our role—has to be believable if we want to create and drive the best story possible. From the dead body under the sheet to the lead actor with 80 percent of the lines, every role can have an impact. There are no small parts, only small, unbelievable actors who aren't bringing everything they have to offer to their roles.

Don't let that be you. Show up as your wonderful self and win your fellow players over. Leverage who you are to make an impact. Contribute your unique value to the story. And then watch as your personal storyline becomes more exciting and inspiring.

CHAPTER 4

EMBODY YOUR CHARACTER— YOUR PRESENCE

"Before you get into the mind, you have to
inhabit the physicality. Body language is a great
way of speaking."[24]—MICHELLE YEOH

I heard him coming down the hall before I saw him: Stomp. Stomp. Stomp. The walls shook and the door rattled. I was reminded of "Jack and the Beanstalk" and the terrifying appearance of the giant. I could almost hear the rumbling voice: "Fee. Fi. Fo. Fum."

Of course, it wasn't the giant. It was just "the boss"—Sean—walking back to his office, where I was waiting to meet with him. He appeared around the hallway corner, striding up the aisle, passing members of his team working hard in their cubicles, never looking left or right, never shifting the "serious" expression on his face.

I felt anxious just watching him.

Once we said hello and he got settled behind his desk, I asked him what was wrong. "Nothing," he said, looking at me quizzically.

"Is this the way you always walk through the office?"

"What do you mean?"

Before I could help myself, I told him how his presence had made me feel. "Watching you walk here, through the office, left

"

me feeling stressed and worried," I said. "I assumed you weren't looking forward to our meeting." Sean was taken aback, and not only because he usually showed up so scary, no one dared to give him feedback.

"Not at all," he told me. "I'm excited to work with you." A good thing, because he had no idea how little his body language reflected what was actually happening for him internally. Worse, his body language wasn't reflecting how he wanted to show up in his role as a leader, how he wanted to bring who he was at his core to the moment. Sean's Power Words were intrepid (his dad had been in the Navy) and significance, openness, growth. I suppose he was being significantly and openly scary, but I'm sure that wasn't what he was going for. He told me that he liked to roll up his sleeves and be with his team in the scrum. He wanted them to see him as a leader and a team player. Instead his body language was making them scared to look him in the eye. The stomping was just one part of the problem, but it was indicative of an "I'm too busy and harried to slow down and engage positively with the world around me" presence.

"What do you think openness or a focus on growth might look like in your expression?" I asked him.

They say awareness is the first step. In this case awareness would help with all Sean's steps. The next time we met, I watched him make his way through the office with a slight smile rather than a slight frown. He stopped to say a few encouraging words to a couple of employees who had their heads together over some problem. And then he glided into the room to meet with me. He had shifted his presence from a scary giant to a purpose-driven, approachable leader and a great player coach.

Whether it's your tone when you're sharing an idea with a colleague, how you stand when presenting in front of 600 people at a sales conference, your facial expressions during virtual meetings, or how you express emotion and leverage your energy to influence your team, your physical presence is a big part of the difference between how you want to show up and how you actually show up. I can't tell you how many times I've been hired to help someone with their "presence" just for us to discover together that all they needed was "permission" and strategies to be more of their true self. Or said differently, how you show up in all ways physical should align with who you are at your core.

Imagine for a minute an actor not paying attention to their character's physicality, tone of voice, or style of speaking—when an actor's primary job is to make their character's whole presence believable and natural to the character's core. Think of the legendary Robert De Niro in *Raging Bull*, Alan Rickman as Professor Snape in the *Harry Potter* films, and Meryl Streep in just about anything, but her role in *The Devil Wears Prada* definitely comes to mind. Her icy, judgmental stare and prowling movements were perfectly vicious and perfectly Miranda Priestly. We believe those actors in their films or onstage, not just because of the words they say, but because of the intentional choices they make about how to fully embody their characters.

In real life, the people all around us perceive us as whole, multi-dimensional beings, and when those dimensions don't align, we end up with a believability gap.

Most of us know that voice, expression, and body language matter. And with the increase in virtual communication, most of us are sensing how much they can matter. Whether we're online or in person, we might know to look somebody in the eye or sit up straight to convey confidence and engagement. And one of the questions I'm asked the most by my clients when we are working on how they show up in meetings or on stage is, "Pam, what do I do with my hands?" Seriously. When people start becoming more conscious of the "character" they want to play—their true, core character—they start becoming more self-conscious of their physical behavior and presence. But self-conscious is not the same thing as self-aware.

Few of us are taught to be fully aware of and intentional with what we're doing with our bodies and our expressions, especially when we're in the hotseat, under pressure or dealing with a difficult situation. We don't realize how much our physical presence reveals about what's happening for us internally—or how often we're sending miscues about what's happening. And how many of us have been taught how to translate who we fundamentally are and how we want to show up in the world into our stance, tone of voice, expression, or energy? The lucky few who get a presentation or media coach? People who took some acting classes for fun in college?

In this chapter, I want to help you shift from being *un*aware or self-*conscious* to being *self-aware and intentional*, so that you can feel comfortable, confident, and have a powerful impact on people and your environment with your entire being. You'll learn techniques and tools that can help you convey who you are, what you think and believe, and your passion using the best tool of all—you!

Leveraging Your Presence
to Be More Believable

One of my biggest laughs with a client happened in my first session, my first ten minutes, with Lauren. "Oh yeah, I worked with someone like you, a communication coach who was supposed to prep me for my speech at a big sales conference," she said. "Our sales were down significantly, and the coach told me to hold out my hand"—she demonstrated for me—"and as I said 'sales…are…down' raise my hand *higher* with each word. She said the audience would pay more attention to my hand than my words and walk away imagining sales going up." She paused. "Isn't that dumb?"

Yup.

I knew where that coach was getting inspiration: Professor Albert Mehrabian's work on the importance of nonverbal cues. His research showed that when our words and body language aren't aligned, the nonverbal cues will win in the minds of our audience. However, he was specifically researching in-person communication about feelings, emotions, and attitudes where the words and non-verbal cues don't align. In those situations, people will base their interpretation of our intent on this equation—55 percent on what they see (body language and facial expressions), 38 percent on what they hear (tone of voice), and 7 percent on the words themselves.[25]

Imagine someone saying, "I'm not mad" while crossing their arms, scowling, and muttering. Are you going to believe what they say or what you see and hear? That's what Mehrabian was proving. But that's *all* he was proving. He certainly didn't intend us to use his research to manipulate people into believing something that isn't true! Instead, let's use it as a reminder of how important it is to align our nonverbal cues with who we really are and what we actually want.

What Mehrabian's work does prove is that paying attention to the fundamentals of presence—physicality, voice, expressiveness—is key to bridging the believability gap. Because aligning *perceptions* of our intent based on nonverbal cues with our *actual* intent has a big impact on whether people trust us or not, and how believable we are.

In Lauren's case, wouldn't it have been better to use her presence to communicate that despite a downward trend in sales, she was a deep believer in the members of her team and their products and was committed to their success? Because all of that was true! And she would have honestly and genuinely leveled up the confidence of the audience. When I asked her how she would have liked to present the news, she did the most marvelous thing. She immediately stepped forward, toward her "audience" (always a sign of connection), and put her hands together in a sort of prayer pose. Then she spoke with compassion and emotion about how much she appreciated them and had faith in them. What a powerful impact she could have had!

Actors use so many methods (no pun intended) and consider so many attributes to ensure the physical believability of their characters. They spend years on vocal training. They take classes in Alexander Technique, a way of changing unconscious body and movement habits that create unnecessary tension and poor posture. They play with the Lecoq method, wearing masks so they only have their bodies to express specific emotions and ideas. They practice the Chekhov technique of conveying emotions through gestures, which I'll describe more below. I needed all of that practice and coaching, because while I was great at the intellectual work of acting—character studies, research, and even just learning lines—my directors and teachers kept telling me the same thing. "Remember, your character has a body!"

Actors are simply trying to physically and expressively reflect the personality, lived experiences, and varied emotional states of a character to create a whole, believable portrayal. Two amazing recent examples come from the movie *Mickey 17* and the series *Severance*. Both give us an opportunity to watch the same actor show up physically different to convey variations on the same character. In *Mickey 17*, Robert Pattinson plays two versions of a clone—one mild-mannered and agreeable, the other mildly psychotic and violent. When we see them onscreen together, we can immediately tell them apart—by posture, expression, voice, cadence, and how each of them moves—even though they fundamentally look the same. And in *Severance*, we can watch actors change so many aspects of their physical presence as they shift between playing "innies" and "outies"—their character in the highly manipulated workplace and their character in the outside world, with no memories shared between them.

I'm not asking you to try to play two different versions of yourself! I'm asking you to do the opposite and consider subtle, intentional adjustments you can make that will align your presence with your core character.

Be Still. Be Aware.

To be more believable to others, you've got to play the hokey pokey and put your whole self in. The first step is getting to know your instrument—your body. And the best way to do that is to practice neutrality, or stillness.

One of my favorite roles was playing the character Liz Imbrie in Philip Barry's *The Philadelphia Story*—the classic play that became a movie with Katharine Hepburn, Cary Grant, and Jimmy Stewart. Liz is the photographer who is assigned to take pictures of the Philadelphia socialite—she is an observer, albeit an observer who interjects the best acerbic comedic lines in the play. I'm a kinetic actor—I like to move around the space—and that wasn't going to work for this role. So my director gave me a goal—to not move for as long as possible. The stillness required to be an observer who was cooking up those zingers was hard for me, and I had to work on making that stillness look natural. I wasn't supposed to look like I was holding myself still, tightly controlled. I was supposed to look nonchalant, in keeping with the character's "I don't care" attitude about life.

To prepare before every show, I would do what I call the stillness exercise. I teach it to most of my clients—and now to you—as an important starting point because it does three things.

* It releases stress, calming your body and your mind.
* It helps you learn how to be more aware of your body and how it feels in different states of being. When you become familiar with what it feels like to be neutral, you become more aware when you're not neutral.
* It grounds you and allows you to find a position of neutrality. From there, you can make more intentional choices about your movements and your energy, using your body to convey what you mean or intend instead of letting it unconsciously convey…whatever.

You're going to breath tension in and out of your body, to work on the mind-body connection. With each breath in you'll put tension into a specific body part, and with each breath out you'll release that tension. Let's begin.

Be Still

- Sit on a chair with everything unfolded. Don't twist your legs or arms up like a pretzel. Put your feet firmly on the floor. Adjust your posture until you feel comfortable and neutral. Lay your hands in your lap.

- Close your eyes and take a deep breath.

- Starting at your feet, focus your attention there. Take a deep breath in and as you do, tense the muscles. As you exhale, release the tension. Next, move up to your calves and do the same, then your thighs (and as a result your gluteus maximus), your stomach, your chest, your arms, and your face, breathing in tension, breathing out release.

- When you've moved through each part of your body, take one big breath in and imagine it flowing through your entire body and gathering any tension that's still lingering. Then imagine there's a spout at the top of your head and as you exhale, send all the tension out too.

- Remain sitting for at least thirty seconds, breathing in and out, and get familiar with what stillness and your body feel like.

Imagine doing this exercise before you have a difficult conversation with a colleague so that you can make intentional choices about how to hold yourself, how to maintain an open expression, or how to control your gestures to get to the best outcome. Or before a performance review meeting—being still can show up as confidence and is useful when you feel anxious or are worried about becoming defensive. Or even before you celebrate a big win with the team, so that you can raise your physical energy in the moment to show your joy, excitement, and pride in a way that flows through the room. These are the kinds of intentional, aligned, believability building choices we can all make—and that start with body awareness and centering.

What you do next is up to you and your Power Words.

Power Words in Motion

I learn so much about people by watching how they move through their workspaces and offices and interact with others, like I had with Sean. And like I did with Remi.

Remi was a former Army officer turned physician. He was smart and compassionate and fundamentally good at his job—but that's not what he was known for. If you asked most people who worked with him to use one word to describe him, it would probably have been *disorganized* or *harried*. As I sat in a conference room waiting for him, I watched him sprint through the office, literally leaping over anything in his way. He slammed into the glass door, hurtled to a chair, and then looked at me expectantly, breathless, ready to wrestle his believability to the ground. Exhausting!

Remi's core defining word was "selfless" and his character beliefs were "integrity," "compassion," and "connectedness." "Do you believe that it's selfless to rush from meeting to meeting, to show up breathless and seemingly distracted? Do you believe that people feel your compassion if you're moving so fast you can't actually look them in the eye? If you want to be believable as who you are at your core, you're going to have to slow down," I told him.

The whole point of choosing your Power Words is to show up as yourself—through your behavior and presence. Amy Cuddy, author of *Presence*, wrote that it's "the state of being attuned to and able to comfortably express our true thoughts, feelings, values, and potential."[26] Remi's values were clear to him and he had massive potential, but his presence wasn't attuned to these facets of who he was.

I know I asked you to put your Power Words on a Post-it note, but that's not where they should live. To truly evoke and convey your Power Words, you have to intentionally embody them and bring them to life. So, how would you walk if, say, "integrity" is one of your core beliefs? Would you be more deliberate? Would you pay more attention to your environment and the people in it? Would you stand a little taller because you've got *integrity* running through the core of your body? My core word is energy. You can bet that when I'm in front of an audience, I'm not standing still and speaking in a monotone. And I actually stand whenever I'm presenting in a virtual setting to ensure that my core defining word can shine through that screen.

To help him convey his Power Words through his body, I gave Remi an assignment, and I'm going to give you the same one.

Your Power in Your Presence

1. First, a journal assignment. Consider your Power Words and spend some time contemplating and writing down your thoughts on the following questions:

   - What do you think are some of the physical behaviors that convey these values or ideals? Why?

   - Where do you think your presence is misaligned with your Power Words? Why do you think so?

2. Next, look for inspiration from the world of intentional character development.

    • Try to think of a television or film character who you think most embodies each of your Power Words. For instance, Harvey Specter in *Suits* seems to have bravado running through him. Jack Pearson in *This Is Us* exudes love through his physical presence.

    • Once you've chosen a character, spend some time watching them with the sound off. Pay attention to how they're *being*, not what they're saying. Make notes about what you notice in their physical presence. I don't want you to mimic them, but I do want you to think about the intentional choices the actor made about how to convey that value or character trait.

3. Consider the power of a *psychological gesture*. This is an idea developed by the great Michael Chekhov. An actor turns a character's vital want or need into a physical gesture and then practices it over and over until it becomes internalized rather than exaggerated, an internal emotional state aligned with an external physical movement. Is there a small, simple physical habit you could develop that conveys one of your Power Words? Is there a physical habit you should change because it's getting in the way of your Power Words?

4. Finally, decide what you will do differently going forward. How could your core defining word or your character beliefs better influence your body language throughout the day? How will you shift your presence to align it with how you want to live your Power Words?

Your Uniquely Powerful Voice

Eliza was an introvert—or at least that's how she introduced herself in our very first conversation. She was skeptical about working with me, and I understood why. "I like to do my job quietly," she said. And I had been tasked by Eliza's director with helping her speak up more or to "find her voice."

I don't like that phrase, find your voice. It implies that some people have lost their voice or never had one. That's not the problem. The challenge is developing the internal belief that you should use your voice, that you have a lot to offer through it, and that it's an important tool for revealing who you are to the world around you.

In the Tarzan movie, *Greystoke*, Andie MacDowell played Jane. She was twenty-three years old, and it was her big break, her very first role in a film. It had an incredible, award-winning cast and was being directed by Hugh Hudson, who had just won an Academy Award for *Chariots of Fire*. But after filming ended, the team decided that her southern accent was too pronounced and they hired Glenn Close to dub the entire movie, without telling Andie until it was done and the movie was just about to release. She has described it as a shocking, devasting experience. "I was dead, basically, as an actor."[27] Her confidence was so rocked, she couldn't actually speak when her agent wanted to contest the decision. But eventually, she focused on the legacy she wanted to leave, fought for her career, and embraced her authentic, beautiful, lilting voice. Today, that's how we know her and it's an avenue for her power.

"Eliza, your voice is uniquely yours," I told her. "It doesn't have to be loud. In fact, sometimes a quiet voice is the one everyone stops to listen to. Think about what your colleagues might be missing by not hearing what you have to offer." We started by setting a simple goal. Eliza would say something at every meeting. Even if it was just to say, "I agree." She needed to get used to hearing the sound of her voice in a room with more than one other person in it—and learn to love it.

Beyond building belief in the value of using your voice, it's important to understand what makes a voice powerful. Because in real life, there's no one to dub it. It's up to you to use your unique voice to grow your believability with audiences. How? Actors pay attention to vocal qualities like tone, cadence, pitch, pace, energy, emphasis, and even the power of the pause.

I spent hours and hours mastering Erma Bombeck's voice, which was very different from my own. She was born and raised in Ohio. I'm a born and bred New Yorker. I had to learn how to say "cottage cheese" like an Ohioan. (Although, mastering her voice was a lot easier than the voice I never quite mastered when doing a voice over for a relaxation video. That's not easy for somebody whose core defining word is *energy*.) Of course there are recordings of her voice, and I listened to them. But I didn't try to mimic it. Instead, I thought about how I, as an actor on stage, could convey something important about who she was through her voice. I thought about her beliefs of family, humor, and grace. I felt what formed her voice at a basic level was a warm smile, and that's what I worked on rather than trying to replicate exactly how she spoke.

Just like any actor, maximizing your influence and impact through your voice requires you to be thoughtful about its effect on others. We've known for decades how important tone is in our ability to connect with, persuade, and be believable to others. One study found that Kickstarter campaigns were more successful when the entrepreneurs in the videos conveyed focus, low stress, and emotional stability through their vocal tone. It made people believe in their competence.[28] Just through tone, we can change the implicit meaning people attach to words and how they remember them.[29]

Your voice is the tool by which your character comes to life for other people. Get to know it and be intentional about being more believable through it.

Understanding the Potential and Power of Your Unique Voice

Likely, you have recordings of your voice available to you. Because of how much time we all spend in virtual meetings, many of which are recorded, you might have a gold mine of research material to pull from. And if you don't, you can start creating it now. Simply record some of your meetings.

Now comes the less comfortable part. Listen to the recordings and focus on your voice. Knowing what your voice sounds like when you are unconsciously using it allows you to start making intentional choices about how to use it.

As you listen, reflect on the following questions:

- What do you notice about your pace, your cadence, your tone, how you use emphasis, and any other attributes of your voice and speaking style?

- Are there moments when you feel you sound more like "you." Why? What's different? What do you like about different aspects of your voice or speech in those moments?

- Are there moments when you don't? And why?

- At any peak moments in the meeting or conversation or speech, do you feel your vocal energy and tone reflected what you wanted to bring to the meeting? Did they help you get closer to your goal or build connection with your audience?

Learn to Breathe

The first exercise I asked you to do in this chapter required you to breathe in a very specific way, with intention. And in this section, I'm going to ask you to do the same, with a different purpose in mind.

Of course, you already know how to breathe. You do it unconsciously every moment of the day. But most of us breath shallowly, and so we lose the power of one of our greatest tools of presence, our voice. Just as important, strong, deep, restorative breathing has amazing physical and mental health benefits. In his massive bestseller *Breath*, James Nestor summarized his years of research and interviews and personal experiences: "Yes, how we breathe really does affect the size and function of our lungs. Yes, breathing allows us to hack into our own nervous system, control our immune response, and restore our health. Yes, changing how we breathe will help us live longer.... The missing pillar in health is breath. It all starts there."[30]

Eliza told me that when she *did* choose to speak in meetings, she had trouble being heard, even in online meetings where she had a mike! She was constantly being told to speak up and she felt it was hurting perceptions of the value of what she had to say—and I'm sure her believability. Rather than asking her to speak, I asked her to show me how she was *breathing*. I watched as she almost hyperventilated, her chest rising higher and higher as she took a deep breath. I knew we could change her confidence and presence with a simple exercise.

Consider how many times you've run out of breath in the middle of a big pitch or at a meeting when emotions were running high, leaving you sounding out of control rather than in control, or weak instead of strong in your opinion. Actors train their voices by training their breath first to creating a belief-building voice. Learning how to strengthen your diaphragm and lungs will support your breath, steady your voice, grow your vocal energy, and allow you to be more intentional with your volume, your points of emphasis, your cadence, and more.

A Stronger Voice with Belly Out Breathing

- Lie down flat on the floor with your knees up so that your back is flat on the floor.

- Breathe in for a count of ten and while you do, push your belly out. Hold the breath and the position for ten seconds.

- Slowly breathe out for a count of at least ten and don't let your belly collapse. I know, it's not easy.

- Keep doing this exercise, day after day, steadily increasing the time it takes to release the breath while still holding your belly out.

- When you feel your breath and belly are more in control, practice the exercise while standing. It will give you the ability to prep your voice no matter where you are, with every breath you take.

Using Your Voice—and Face—to Be Wonderfully, Believably Expressive

All of this work on voice and body language is really about how you can express yourself believably by bringing core elements of your character to life. And the next step in that journey is actually being *expressive*. What do I mean? Think about reading aloud to a child, and try to remember how fun it can be. Trying out funny voices. Laughing together at the ridiculous lines. Being wonderfully expressive and energetic to create a compelling performance. Do you remember how the kids responded? They were rapt, right?

Now compare that to the last time you heard a colleague open a meeting by saying "I'm so excited to be here" in a flat monotone, without energy. Not fun, and not believable. I don't want that to be you. I don't want you to be an animatronic robot like the ones at Disney. My mission is for you to be who you are wherever you are in order to ignite your audience. That requires bringing the full range of expressiveness to your entire presence for your audiences, but especially your voice. And again, it requires intentionality.

Why does this matter so much? An article in *Psychology Today* captured it perfectly: "Whatever the content of the things we say, it's our *tone* that communicates what we're feeling when we say them. Our tone tells the truth even when our words don't, even when we're unaware of that truth ourselves. And it's our tone to which others respond."[31] So much of our tone has to do with the emotion we're conveying, intentionally or not. And here's a fascinating bit of neuroscience. Your tone of voice is modulated by the vagus nerve, which runs from your brain stem to your colon. It's part of the parasympathetic nervous system, which automatically controls your heart rate, immune response, digestion. It also plays a role in mood regulation and stress response. Unsurprisingly, your tone of voice can sometimes feel automatic or out of your control. And it makes sense that it will be influenced by your state of mind and whether you're sensing threats or rewards in your environment. All the more reason to be vigilant about it.

One of my favorite things to do with people who we tend to think of as reserved or introverted, like engineers, data analysts, or accountants is to have them read short poems by Shel Silverstein, author of *Where the Sidewalk Ends* and *The Giving Tree*, while trying to convey a specific emotion. It's a little weird and uncomfortable but they're often more expressive with each other than they've ever been before! In the next exercise, I'm going to ask you to do similar work on being expressive. Because as the great actor Sir Derek Jacobi once said, you can use the power of your voice "to lift the words off the page and inhabit them and give them a soul and a sense of feeling and a life."[32]

Building Expressiveness in Your Voice

- Find a picture book, maybe your favorite, and one with more than one character.

- Read it out loud without paying attention to your voice.

- Next, read it aloud again, but this time "do all the voices," as my kids used to say. How did that feel? What did you notice?

- Then—and this is the fun part—choose one of your Power Words and consider how you would convey it through your voice. Would your cadence change? Would you increase your speed to convey energy (but don't go too fast!)? Would you vary your tone or pitch to convey excitement? Now, read the book out loud again in that voice. What did you hear? How did it feel?

You can expand and enhance your believability with the powerful tools you've been given that are uniquely yours—your body, your voice, your expression, your very presence. You don't have to be an actor to use them for inspiration and influence. All it takes is a little awareness and some intentional choices. Try it in your next meeting or conversation and see what happens! I'm certain that by paying attention to all that the "whole" you has to offer, you'll be more believable to you and to others.

PART 2

Dream, Craft, and Share Your Character's Story

CHAPTER 5

THE STORY OF YOUR FUTURE

"Stories help us believe in possibility."[33]—Viola Davis

Imagine a world...
What happened for you when you read that line? Where did your brain go? I bet it didn't go to the negative, did it? Did your thinking expand into the wide, open future? Did you feel yourself relax a bit as your brain shifted away from the worries of the present? Did you feel a little burst of curiosity and excitement?

This is the power dreaming carries in our lives. It's why I've always been fascinated by actors—they are dreamers at heart. Dreaming allows us to create a story of the future different and better than the present. Brian David Johnson, a futurist and innovation specialist who has worked with companies like Intel and is now futurist in residence at Arizona State University's Center for Science and the Imagination, said it beautifully: "The way that you change the future is you change the story that people tell themselves about the future they will live in.... If you can change that story, people will actually make different decisions."[34]

Innovators and inventors and leaders do this all the time to build support for their ideas and plans. But any of us can leverage the power of visionary storytelling in our own lives to bridge the believability gap, elevate our impact, and achieve more of what we want. That's what I want to help you do in this chapter.

Amina Slaoui is an inspiring example of what can happen when we do.

In 1992, while traveling through Paris on their way to a holiday in Central America, Amina and her husband Ibrahim unexpectedly found themselves in the middle of a large demonstration of people with disabilities, rallying for their rights. She remembers feeling such empathy for the protesters. Little did she know that less than three weeks later she would be facing the same struggles.

She and her husband were on a bike trip in a remote area of Costa Rica when Amina fell off a bridge into a ravine. She knew almost immediately that she would never walk again. It took fifteen hours for her to be rescued and transported to a hospital in the capital city, San José. She was lucky to even survive the journey, but she faced a much longer journey into a life that had been changed forever.

Amina was eventually moved to the Mayo Clinic's rehabilitation center in Rochester, Minnesota. There, she discovered the power of making patients active participants in their rehabilitation planning and process, and it was empowering. They showed patients what might be possible in their new lives, they treated them as experts in their own lives, and they addressed both the physical and psychological aspects of recovery. Two months later, she moved to a rehabilitation center in Paris and finally to another one in Montpellier, France. There, she was closer to her family and friends in Morocco, where she and her husband lived with their two young children.

During her time in the hospital, she began to focus on the future. "How am I going to adapt the best way I can?" she thought. "I want to be proud of myself, I want my children to be proud of me, and I want to *do* something." She was a highly educated entrepreneur, a mother, and a wife. She wanted to lead a full life, she wanted to have more children, and she wanted to make a difference, she told me when I interviewed her for a global leadership conference more than a decade ago. And that's the story she began to tell herself and others—which allowed her to start making a difference just four months after her accident.

At the hospital in Paris, she saw a problem in the way patients were treated. The head of the rehabilitation program was arrogant and believed his job was to tell patients what to do. Their job was to just do it. That thinking spread throughout the program. She needed to change *his* mind first. She volunteered for experimental treatments with him so that she could build a connection. Then, she began describing her experiences at the Mayo Clinic and what a difference it had made in her recovery. By the time she left, she had organized a mini-conference for the doctors and assistants where she educated them on a better, more empowering approach to working with patients.

When she returned home to Morocco, six months after her injury, she discovered new obstacles. Trying to go out and about with her family was difficult because Morocco was so hard to navigate in a wheelchair. Worse, people with disabilities in Morocco were invisible. You didn't see them on the streets, in shops, or in restaurants.

While she was in hospital, Amina had received a letter introducing her to Mohamed El Khadiri, who had also been paralyzed in an accident and had gone on to found the Amicale Marocaine des Handicapés (now Groupe AMH) to advocate for others like him. She met with him soon after returning home. As a prominent business leader and entrepreneur, Amina was influential in Morocco and she could leverage her influence to bring about change. She began by organizing fundraisers and working to bring people with disabilities into society. Together, she and Mohamed crafted a vision of tackling the greatest hurdle: a rehabilitation hospital where people could get the life saving and life changing treatment they needed without having to leave Morocco. And in just a couple of years, despite all kinds of hurdles, the hospital became a reality—the Noor Hospital Center in Casablanca. It offers rehabilitation, vocational training, psychological and social supports, training for professionals, and more. And I got to visit it in Morrocco—it can be truly astonishing to see someone's vision realized in bricks and mortar.

Over the next thirty years, Amina became the president of Groupe AMH, dramatically expanded its reach and impact, took on a primary school of 580 kids where 20 percent of the students have a disability, and has won numerous awards for her advocacy efforts. "My dream," she said in an interview in 2023 for Harvard Business School, "is to live in a world where disability is not an exception but part of our beautiful diversity. I dream for a world that embraces us."[35] When I asked her recently about what drove her early on, her answer was simple—love. That sounds like a pretty powerful Why to me.

Amina is one of the most inspiring people I know, and the embodiment of the idea that when we create our own vision of the future, we give ourselves a north star that influences how we see ourselves and how others see us. *When we create a story of our future that's so powerful we don't want to hold back, can't wait to share it out loud, we inspire ourselves and others to start out on a journey. And then our behaviors in the present begin to change.* We become more believable because we're clear about where we're going and we're more likely to make decisions and take actions that are aligned with that vision.

Actors do this for the characters they play. They know that to be believable, they need to connect the present and future for the audience, through what they do and say, how they show up on stage or on set. So they visualize the character's future and use it to make intentional choices about what the character should be doing in the present to achieve that future.

Too often, especially in the world of our work, we let go of this important aspect of our own believability by tamping down our dreams instead of tapping into them. To be more *you* on the stage of your life, to close the believability gap, you need a clear sense of where you're going, and you need to be able to convey that in a way that's compelling to yourself and others, as a story. *Because a dream is just a story that hasn't been written yet. You get to write yours.*

In this part of the book, we'll start with the power of your future, then we'll uncover stories from your past—your character's backstory—that you can share to create a throughline, and finally I'll help you turn those important throughline moments into compelling stories you can share to build engagement and connection. Some people I work with end up refining their visions once they do the work of exploring their throughline. Stories from the past offer insights into our strengths, talents, and true passions, which can impact our vision of where we want to go next. Be prepared to come back to different exercises to refine and clarify.

For now, let's dive into vision. Crafting it isn't difficult. I would argue that yours is already living inside of you. I'll guide you through the kinds of work actors do to build their imagination muscles and become story thinkers so that you can envision a future for your character and then share it in a compelling way that motivates you and builds a connection between you and the people in your life. Because story is the chalice from which you can fill your believability cup.

And keep this in mind as we go: Your vision is only as emotionally compelling to other people as it is to you. How strongly you believe in it, how well you can envision it, and how well you can tell the story of it influences how believable you'll be in communicating it to others.

A Vision for the Future
Could Change Your Life

The award-winning writer Brian Ackley once explained that "an invested actor will dream of the world you've created for their character."[36] It's not unusual for an actor to develop their character's backstory and future story when they aren't fully developed by the writer. Even when they know the future that's being laid out in the script, actors will go on a journey to understand how their character evolves to achieve that future, how they become more themselves (in the case of positive evolution). They do this to enhance their portrayal of the character, to be more believable. In his MasterClass on acting, Samuel L. Jackson described the draw of the future story in creating a compelling character that audiences want to know more about: "Whenever you're on stage, you're coming from somewhere and you're going somewhere when you leave. And do you want people to go with you?"[37] It's conveying that future in how he portrays the character that make audiences want to follow him when he leaves.

The future story is even more powerful when the character is driven by a vision. The characters from some of the most seminal movies of our time had visions that shaped who they are and our journey with them—from Rocky the boxer, to a hobbit with a quest, to a high school principal trying to improve his underperforming school, to a basketball team from a small town trying to win the championship. It's their visions for the future that make them so watchable, inspiring, and engaging. And the actors who portray them need to connect deeply with that drive for a better future to convey commitment, focus, dedication, and joy—real joy.

Many of the characters we find compelling, that we follow, that we feel connected to, and that we believe in *aren't* fictional. Think of visionaries like Steve Jobs and Bill Gates but also people like Brené Brown. They tell us stories that help us believe in a better possible future, and they do it by sharing a specific and intentional story of the future they're trying to create. Because as I wrote at the beginning of this chapter, that's how you change people's behavior and how you change the world—your world.

Science and research back this up. A powerful vision boosts our motivation specifically because it creates a *vivid mental picture of a future reality.* Visions boost our mood and optimism about the future, they focus our efforts so that we accomplish more, and they motivate us to achieve goals. And even if we are taken off our path unexpectedly by difficult life events, reconnecting with or crafting a new vision can get us back on our path to finding happiness. It can restore our sense of self.[38] I think Amina would attest to that.

Every one of us has been inspired and engaged by somebody else's vision. We've felt a deep emotional connection when we watch them go on the journey to achieve it. So why—*why*—is it so hard to recognize the power that vision can have in our own lives? When I'm working with teams and executives, the moment I say the word vision, I get eye rolls or glassy eyed stares. It makes me want to shake people because I've seen what happens to people and teams when they lack vision. And I've seen what's possible when they can tell a powerful story of their future.

A vision is much more than a goal. In their bestseller *Switch*, a book all about positive change, Chip Heath and Dan Heath explained that even well-constructed goals "*presume* the emotion; they don't generate it."[39] A vision generates the positive emotional engagement, and we need that if we want to make progress. It tells the rational side of your mind where you're going and the emotional side "why the journey is worthwhile." And it boosts your believability by being inspiring and engaging to other people's emotion-driven brains, too!

Our visions have the power to *pull* us into the future of our choosing. Robert Fritz and Peter Senge did important research on this. Fritz is a management consultant, a composer, and a filmmaker who focuses on creativity. Senge is a management guru, systems scientist, and professor at the MIT Sloan School of Management. In *The Fifth Discipline*, Senge shared a powerful concept based on their work: creative tension.

People often have great difficulty talking about their visions, even when the visions are clear. Why? Because we are acutely aware of the gaps between our vision and reality.… But the gap between vision and current reality is also a source of energy. If there was no gap, there would be no need for any action to move toward the vision. Indeed, the gap is the source of creative energy. We call this gap creative tension.

Imagine a rubber band, stretched between your vision and current reality. When stretched, the rubber band creates tension, representing the tension between vision and current reality. What does tension seek? Resolution or release.…

It's not what the vision is, it's what vision does.[40]

A strong vision that we commit to sets our subconscious to work, trying to figure out how to relieve that tension and achieve that vision. Without a clear vision, you miss out on that creative tension and the motivation for change and progress.

To make the vision compelling, you have to be able to visualize it. Actors get this. It's part of their daily work to develop and leverage creative tension. They exercise their imagination and visualization muscles to create a vision that allows them portray a character believably—internally and externally—and that helps them pull the audience into their imagined world.

So let's start by working out *your* muscles.

Strengthening Your Vision Muscle

Michael was a research and development engineer at a pioneering medical device company that was all about vision. He was also incredibly harried and overworked. It wasn't who he was at his core, or how he wanted to show up, but he couldn't seem to pull himself out of the daily mire. He couldn't let go and delegate, and it was affecting how he led and the impact he was having on his team. His boss could see he was fraying around the edges and asked me to work with him. True to what I had been told, every time we would meet he would spend twenty minutes debriefing me on the gazillion things he was working on, large and small. He was so zoomed in on the tasks in front of him—and there were plenty of them, far more than there needed to be—that developing a vision was the last thing on his to do list. It wasn't even *on* the list. But he was missing a north star that would help him prioritize. Until he had it, he wouldn't be able to focus on bigger and better possibilities for the future.

When we are so zoomed in on what's happening now, of course it feels like the future will be more of the same. We have a hard time imagining something greater or even different. Often we feel we simply don't have the time to step back, zoom out, and craft a vision that might guide us in the present. We don't recognize that an inspiring vision can help us focus, prioritize, make more strategic decisions about where and how to use our time and energy.

So before we think about specifics, let's work on building our vision muscle, our capacity for dreaming. Proving that you're capable of achieving more than you might think is a good way to start exercising your vision muscle and start breaking down unnecessary limits on your vision. When you dream, there should be no constraints.

To expand your brain's perception of what's possible and overcome limiting thoughts, try what I call the finger pointing exercise.

The Pointing Exercise

- Stand in the middle of a room, where you have a bit of space. Raise your dominant arm straight in front of you and point your finger.

- Now, keeping your feet firmly in place, twist to that side as far as you can go, keeping your arm out straight. When you've really, truly gone as far as you can, make a note of what you're pointing at—a doorframe, a picture, a mark on the wall—and face front again.

- Now, keep your arm raised and close your eyes. Picture the wall you were just pointing at and pick a target that's farther along the wall than the spot you were able to point at. It could be five or even ten inches beyond that spot.

- Keeping your eyes closed, twist in that same direction, again going as far as you possibly can.

- Now open your eyes.

I bet that even if you didn't reach the target you envisioned, you pointed at a spot that's farther than your original spot, that you were able to twist more. Even though you felt you had gone as far as you could go the first time.

With your eyes tight shut, your experience isn't limited by your perceptions of what's possible. And when you free your mind and prove to yourself that "bigger" is possible, you give yourself the courage to dream bigger.

Reconnecting with the Future You

Michael was so immersed in the here and now, I knew there was no hope of helping him craft a powerful story of the future that could inspire him and others until he could connect personally with that future. So I took a risk. "I want you to put absolutely everything away, silence your phone, and close your laptop," I said. His eyes widened, but he did as I asked. "Now I want you to lay down on the floor." I gave him a throw pillow to put under his head. "We're going to go on a journey to meet your future self."

Visualization is a tool actors use all the time. We visualize ourselves on stage or performing a scene. We visualize the world we are building with other actors. And we visualize our character living their life in the past or the future, beyond what we've been told in the script. We're crafting a vivid internal story that will build our believability in our role.

That's what I wanted Michael to do and what I encourage you to do. Learn how to put yourself in the future, to envision it with specificity and intention. There is a part of your brain that is always thinking about the future, already envisioning what it might be like. All you need to do is leverage the power of your imagination to connect with it. Then, you'll motivate yourself to shift your behavior, to align it with how you want to show up going forward to achieve that better future.

Before beginning the next exercise, remember the techniques I described for relaxing and grounding yourself in Chapter 4 by breathing tension into and out of your body. It's a good starting point for any visualization work.

Meet Your Future Self

Find a place and position where you can feel completely relaxed. Once you are, think about a point in the future that's not too far away, maybe a year from now. (A five-year vision can be hard to imagine, let alone accomplish.)

Put yourself into that future moment using all of your senses. Choose a place or even a specific moment. Try to *experience* that future as if it's now.[41]

Reflect on these questions: Where are you? What are you doing? Who are you with? How do you feel? What has changed? How are your Power Words and Power Drivers showing up?

Next, bring yourself back to the present, set a timer for three minutes, and write—with a pen and paper, not a computer! (We process information and ideas differently as we physically write, activating different parts of the brain so that it engages at a deeper level.) Freely write everything you can think of about your future self, everything you imagined, everything you dreamed. Not sure how to begin? Try describing something physical, like what you were doing, what you were wearing, a list of the people with you, and then expand from there. Capture as much detail as you can. Write without stopping. If the timer goes off and you're still writing, great, but write for at least three minutes.

After I lead people through this exercise I always ask, "How do you feel about the future now?" Their faces light up. Some have tears in their eyes. And that's what happened for Michael. "What did you see that sparked so much emotion?" I asked.

"Time," he said. "I had time." It was the gift his future self had given him. From that moment on, he started to recognize that he was the master of how he spent it. He had the same twenty-four hours each day as everybody else, and he got to choose what to do with it. Suddenly, developing a vision seemed vital because he *wanted* to prioritize, to pay more attention to the things that mattered and let go of the things that didn't.

It's as award-winning actor Colin Farrell once said in an interview, "We are consumed with existence, mortgages, jobs, competition, clothes, cars, houses. It is nice to allow the imagination room to breathe again and see life as something that is spectacular and magic.... Then we can come back into our environment with that gift that we've been bestowed."[42]

When people visualize the future, they're bringing what's already living in their imagination out and into the world. Some have major revelations about what they want and where they're headed, which begin to close internal believability gaps. But most are simply inspired. Because even though we all have worries about the future, no one ever envisions a crappy future. No one.

To See All the Benefits, Craft a Vision That's True to Your Character

Sometimes, even if we think we have a vision, it's a story somebody else told us we should go for. It's disconnected from who we are at our core and based on what other people want for us. Exhibit A: my brief life as a lawyer.

When we fall into that trap, we immediately discount the potential positive effects of having a vision at all! Recently, researchers studied people with stated visions in three related experiments. They were trying to understand why having a vision has a bigger positive impact on some people. For all three experiments, they assessed people's visions for "self-concordance"—how well aligned a vision or goal is with somebody's intrinsic values, beliefs, and interests. They shared their findings in an article for the *Journal of Research in Personality*.[43] In the first experiment, they proved that people with visions that are well-aligned with who they are at their core saw more positive mood and emotional benefits. In the second and third studies, they found that visions with high self-concordance boosted people's commitment to progress on their goals over time.

I wish they had done the research a few decades ago. It might have saved me from some hard years.

Even though I had an early love of performing, I went to college and then onto law school because that's what I was encouraged to do. But as I worked my way through law school and into my early years in corporate law, I just kind of…plodded along. (Except when I was silently screaming at the ceiling, if you recall that vivid scene from Chapter 1.) I believe in doing good work no matter what I'm doing, and I'm a type A high achiever, so I was doing just fine. But I was also mired in the daily grind, increasingly uninspired.

My husband, on the other hand, was fresh out of business school and was all about plans and visions. "Crafting a vision of success is the first step toward success," he would tell me. Beyond being deeply annoying to somebody who couldn't see past the end of the week, it just sounded like greeting card wisdom to me. But one day, he shared the source of this wisdom—a plaque on his boss's desk that said, "Leadership is the ability to communicate a vision and gain commitment to it."

For some reason, I was struck by that simple sentence much more than any of his other advice. Maybe it was the idea of being able to communicate in a way that would build committed followership. Maybe it was that I felt every element—leadership, vision, commitment—was kind of missing from my life. The big revelation was that I'd lost my inspiration precisely because I didn't have a vision, a future story for my own character. Or if I did, it wasn't aligned with who I was at my core. And I probably couldn't be successful as a lawyer because I wasn't excitedly dreaming about that future. I wasn't committed to it. I was just going through the motions.

It took me longer than I like to admit—and more pain than I like to remember—to let a dream I had cultivated from the time I was a little girl, a powerful vision, to motivate me to action. And there was no question that once I started dreaming and acting again, my confidence and believability grew.

It's time to do some serious vision work. But as you go, keep the work you did to understand who you are at your core at the top of your mind. Consider these questions as you craft your vision:

- ★ What does your inner character really want?
- ★ What are the character beliefs that you want to bring to life—through future action?
- ★ How do your Why and How statements, your Power Drivers, translate into a future goal or state that you're ready to go for?

An exciting story of your future is likely something you're already dreaming up, that's already motivating you, that's alive inside you because of who you are. Now it's time to start shouting it from the rooftops.

Crafting Your Vision as a Vivid and Compelling Story

Visions are deeply personal. Every successful vision I've seen has been different in some fundamental ways. To be compelling, they need to be crafted based on what works for the person crafting them. I'm going to share a few approaches that will give you everything you need to craft yours. What I'm mostly going to do is encourage you to think about your vision, whatever it looks like, as a *story*.

Why is story so important? Dr. Paul Zak has studied the neurobiology of storytelling, or how listening to a powerful story influences the brain. He discovered that when we listen to a good, well-told story, the brain releases oxytocin.[44] Dubbed the "love" hormone, it makes us feel safe and connected. It boosts our trust and *belief in* the teller. Our physiological and emotional response to stories makes them one of the most memorable and engrossing forms of communication.

So maybe it's no big revelation that what makes a story compelling also makes a vision compelling, to us and to others.

* A main character to root for—that's you!
* Specific and detailed.
* Intentional and purposeful (it helps to know why we're listening to a story).
* A beginning and an end (and of course a middle) to convey a journey.
* Emotion.

As you work through the exercises in this section, I want you to work on becoming a story thinker. What is a story thinker? Someone who has the ability to connect with, develop, access, and share stories to engage and influence. The most beautifully powerful description of storythinking comes from Angus Fletcher, who has studied neurophysiology, literature, and narrative theory and literally wrote the book on *Storythinking*.

> Storythinking is contemplating why and what if. It's conjecturing from causes to effects. It's envisioning the consequences of different rules for action. It's mentally modeling hypotheticals, possibles, counterfactuals, and other kinds of could happen. It's using our cerebral machinery to stick original characters into never-before storyworlds and speculate on what happens next. It's natural selection, imaginatively accelerated....

With storythinking, our forerunners dreamed up the republics, renaissances, and rocket ships of our today. And with storythinking, we continue on the narrative, inventing political revolutions, artistic movements, and technological contraptions—then plotting out the actions to hammer fantasy and sci-fi into tomorrow's fresh realities.[45]

Recently, I stood at the back of two different conference rooms and listened to two CEOs kick off big company meetings. What better way to do that than with a compelling vision to excite and engage employees and gain their commitment to "fresh realities." Here's what CEO #1 shared. "Our vision is to hit $20 million in revenue growth for the year!" And CEO #2 said, "We're going to improve our manufacturing efficiency and effectiveness so we can get more of our products to market." Compare those so-called visions to the power of what Angus Fletcher described. Why would either of these leaders think that a collection of data points and business outcomes would inspire, excite, or motivate employees?

With a powerful vision, you have an opportunity to expand your influence and your believability. "People don't want more information," wrote Annette Simmons, master of story and author of *The Story Factor*.[46] "They are up to their eyeballs in information. They want *faith*—faith in you, your goals, your success, in the story you tell. It is faith that moves mountains, not facts.… Faith needs a story to sustain it—a *meaningful* story that inspires belief in you." And for that story to be meaningful and powerful and instill belief, it needs to be *true* (false stories fall apart eventually) and you and the people you share it with need to see it.

As you begin the following two exercises, I want you to do the opposite of what the two CEOs did. I want you to draw on the visualization work we did in the last section—when you met your future self—to expand your thinking, draw on all of your sensory imagination, and prime the emotional pump so that you have what you need to turn your vision into a compelling, engaging story that you and others can see. Be intentional. Be specific. Be bold. And remember, it's not what a vision is, it's what it does.

The Give Yourself an A Exercise

This exercise comes from Benjamin Zander, who wrote *The Art of Possibility* with his wife Rosamund Zander. It was one of the seminal books of my life. Embedded in the book is an exercise he used to do with his students at the New England Conservatory at the beginning of every semester—once he realized that setting expectations for the behavior that would give them the highest grade in the class wasn't the best way to help people grow as creative musicians. They needed to do that for themselves.

Following is the exercise he gave his students for developing a vision for their growth and achievement over the year. It made a huge difference in their commitment and dedication—their personal mastery, as Peter Senge would call it. I do it myself at the end of every year before the new year begins, and I want you to do it now.

- Start by giving yourself an A—assume you've actually accomplished a big goal.

- Put yourself into that future, using the visualization strategies you've already learned. Use your senses to fully experience what this future moment looks and feels like.

- Now, focus on what's different. How have you changed? What did it take to get you to this point? What obstacles did you have to overcome?

> • Once you have a strong, clear sense of this future, write yourself a letter from that future point, in the present tense, as if it has already happened. In the letter, write the story of what you've achieved, how it feels, and what it took for you to get there. You don't have to map every step (that's not effective, actually). Instead describe the bigger changes that closed the gap between your current reality and your envisioned future.

Now, with a strong connection to a future goal and a sense of the journey you'll go on to achieve it, I want you to "Imagine a world…." I want you to capture your dream—not for one specific part of your life, but for all parts of your life. Compelling visions encompass more than one goal or one facet of our worlds. They integrate all of the things we want as we move forward, so that nothing important gets left behind as we go.

Your Dream For…

Write your vision for your world using the following prompts. Remember, be specific, emotionally vulnerable, intentional, and make it vivid and colorful to make it engaging.

- My dream for my career is…

- My dream for my family is…

- My dream for my personal growth is…

- My dream for my important relationships is…

●

Could you change your future by telling yourself a different story of the future you'll live in? I believe you could, and the science and research back me up on that. When you write your vision as a powerful, compelling story, you're giving yourself the foundation you'll need to start building internal and external belief in it. Your energy will rise. You'll be able to bring who you are at your core to life through the story. And you'll be prepared to share it out loud. It will be your guide to the future of your own making—one that will grow your belief in yourself and help others believe in you, too. In the next chapter, I'll show you how to build the throughline from your past that makes your vision for the future much more possible.

CHAPTER 6

DISCOVER YOUR THROUGHLINE

"That inner line of effort that guides the actors
from the beginning to the end of the play, we
call continuity or the through-going action. This
through line galvanizes all the small units and
objectives of the play."[47]—Constantin Stanislavski

Jana Jones had gone from being the only employee of a new health tech company to leading a fast-growing team in what seemed like no time at all. She was the CEO of a subsidiary that was doing big, innovative things to make it easier to share patient data and medical records between doctors.

Other than leading a growing team, Jana had a huge list of stakeholders. She reported to a board, she was trying to attract new users (think hospitals and medical groups) as fast as possible, and she had to convince regulators at the state and national level that sharing patient data electronically could be done safely.

We had spent days developing her vision for her team and worked on how she could share it with different audiences. Still, the story was missing something essential. It wasn't saying enough about who *she* was and why the work mattered to her, deeply. It needed a grounding in the past, a throughline for her character that would make it personal, inspiring, and believable at its core. But every time I'd ask the question, "Why do you do what you do?"

she would respond with trite business speak. I had some clues from her Power Words. Her How statement was to use her "smarts" to change healthcare—inspired by her dad always saying, "use your smarts" when she was a kid.

After lots of starts, stops, and faux stories—stories that she thought were expected of her but that didn't reveal why she was the ideal person to lead her team toward her vision—I said, "I think you're holding back. I can tell how much this matters to you, and I think there's a story there." *Finally*, she shared it with me. This is how I remember it:

> Fifteen years ago, I was diagnosed with lymphoma. My children were small, and my husband and I were determined to beat the cancer. We had to go to a lot of doctors, get lots of tests. Every time we went, the doctors or staff would rifle through huge paper medical files searching for information. They'd ask me about my test results or ask me what the prior doctor had to say because they couldn't find the notes in the reams of paper. We had to listen carefully and write everything down in a green journal we brought with us so we could answer their questions—instead of taking the time we needed to ask our own questions. So, I do what I do so no patient has to carry a green journal again.

I sat in silence, moved to tears, feeling her frustrations and passion. It was an emotional story of how she had used her smarts to solve a healthcare problem, why she wanted to solve that problem for others, and the importance of the work she and her team were doing, beautifully and movingly revealed. And I could see how moved she was. "Why have you never shared that story?" I asked. She was ready with all the usual answers I hear: *It's too personal. It's too emotional. I don't think of it in the moment. Why should people care about my experience?* And my favorite: *I might cry.* Because of course, if you cry when speaking to a business audience, the hounds of doom will pounce.

"Consider the software engineers working into the night that might need to hear that story to understand who they're really working for," I told her. "Or the potential customers and partners who connect to the work you're doing because you understand the patient experience from the inside out. And even the potential investors who want to see a CEO who is deeply, personally committed, not simply following good business strategy."

Everyone is a walking compendium of stories. Those stories help us know who we are in the world and believe in ourselves. Stories create a throughline from our past to our present and into the future that helps us compellingly explore and explain who we are, why we do what we do, and why our vision matters to us to others. It's a line we can use to pull the believability gap closed.

In her book *Insight*, psychologist Tasha Eurich wrote about how important it is to look at the "constellation" of our life stories, the shape they make and what we can learn from them. "When we're able to find consistent themes across multiple important events of our lives, we can glean surprising self-insights."[48] That's what finding our throughline gives us—insights into and commitment to who we are at our core. And when we capture our throughline through stories, we have a compelling, trust-building way to do that with others.

What is your throughline? What stories from your past illuminate who you are, how you're trying to show up, and the path you want to take from here? And how could they impact your audience, move them to action, or improve your connection and their belief in you? That's what I'll help you discover in this chapter.

Why We Keep Our Best Stories to Ourselves— and Why We Shouldn't

Actors are taught almost from day one to delve into their character's backstory—the background that influences their decisions, their feelings, their reactions, their thoughts—so that they can make them three-dimensional, real, and believable.

Viola Davis does deep investigation into what brought her characters to this point in time—sometimes factual by reading or watching documentaries about similar people or the real-life person she is portraying and sometimes imagined. "I write a bio of the character," she said in an interview with BAFTA.[49] "I try to fill it up as much as possible. What are her memories? Does she have brothers and sisters? What secrets does she have? What's her favorite color? I do all of that work first." In the film *Doubt*, she played Mrs. Miller, a woman who turns a blind eye to the abuse her son is experiencing. She struggled to understand the character. How could she make that choice? For the first three weeks of filming, she felt she wasn't fully believable. So she went home one night and wrote a one-hundred-page biography of Mrs. Miller, who was actually a somewhat minor character in the film. It was in that backstory that she finally understood that Mrs. Miller felt she had no choice. She believed she was protecting her son from a much bigger threat.[50] And that insight informed everything about how she portrayed the character going forward. It created a throughline.

It makes sense that actors have to look beyond the script to fill in the stories that make their characters come to life off the page, even if the audience never hears those stories. So why do the rest of us have such trouble doing the same? Especially given that we don't even have to make the stories up! Again, we're all a walking compendium of stories. They're right there, waiting to be shared.

When Jana Jones, from the beginning of the chapter, finally shared her story with me and then in a speech at a company meeting, and then to key stakeholders, and then to a *New York Times* reporter, it boosted her believability by communicating her deep connection to the work of the company. But years later, she revealed something to me. "It actually gave me my own power. It almost didn't matter how many times I repeated it, or how I used it, because it was so true to why I was doing what I was doing. It was inside of me, and putting it out there actually made it *stronger* inside of me. It allowed me to not give up. It didn't matter whether I was testifying on Capitol Hill or meeting with a governor or fighting against internet monopolies or talking with a family practice doctor. None of it felt overwhelming because I knew what I wanted and why, which was to get patients' data safely in the hands of their doctors."

It grounded her and guided her at times when she had to make hard decisions or fight important battles or connect with her customers. It boosted her internal and external believability. "It helped me communicate that my purpose was congruent with the decisions I made, the resources I allocated, the battles I chose to pick, the battles I didn't." It created her throughline.

Despite how often we've seen others powerfully share their stories, most of us carry some resistance to sharing our own full story with the world, just like Jana did initially. Some of us don't believe we're good storytellers, so even if we know we have an important story to share, we hold back. I'll share more on how to overcome that challenge in the next chapter. The bigger reason is usually that we don't like to be vulnerable, especially at work, and good stories reveal so much more about us than basic facts. Sometimes we struggle to remember great stories that would reveal who we are or support what we're trying to accomplish, especially on the fly. And we're afraid of boring people with stories they've heard before or that they don't think are relevant. I remind people all the time that we all love hearing meaningful stories again, and often, the people who most need to hear them haven't yet.

I was leading a session on the power of story in leadership for a large, innovative company in Saudi Arabia. I asked key leaders to share a story about a great challenge. The CEO and cofounder of the company, a quiet, thoughtful, and seemingly reserved man, stood up and unexpectedly began pouring out the story of how the company had almost failed immediately after they launched it. He spoke very quietly but with deep emotion and honesty about the incredible obstacles they had had to overcome to save the company—some spawned from their own mistakes and some from external forces. The story was riveting, and when he finished talking, everybody was silent. I could tell that he had never shared it with the people in the room—his entire leadership team.

After the session ended, the chief financial officer came to me with tears in his eyes and said, "Thank you for this time together. I learned so much about my leader and what it took for him to make all our work possible. I had never heard that story before and I feel even more inspired knowing it."

Marshall Ganz, a professor at Harvard's Kennedy School of Government and a storytelling hero of mine, has said, "When we tell our own story, we teach the values that our choices reveal, not as abstract principles, but as our lived experience. We reveal the kind of person we are."[51] And remember the Paul Zak research I shared in the last chapter, proving that when we hear a well told story, we get a boost of oxytocin, the love drug, which makes us feel more connected to the teller.

The CEO in Saudi Arabia had certainly deepened his connection with his team and inspired them by revealing his character beliefs of innovation, commitment, and resilience.

Sometimes in moments like those, there's a part of me that wants to say, "What took you so long? What were you waiting for?" So I'll ask you. What stories are you holding back that could make a real difference—that could move people to tears or to change or to take action? Let's work on getting them out into the world where they can elevate your impact.

The Stories That Tell the World Who You Are

"Pam, I feel like I've lost myself."

Cara was asking me to help her reconnect with herself, her true self. She had recently started a new job leading a team at a university. It was a different environment from the corporate world in which she had spent her whole career. And just a few months before she took the job, she had finalized her divorce after a twenty-year relationship. She was making this big career change while flying solo, without a partner who knew her well and could boost her confidence as she navigated a new culture. She told me she felt adrift, unable to find her footing in life or in work.

Of course, we started with her Power Words and Power Drivers. But as I've said, they're just words on a page unless you bring them to life. I was trying to help her reconnect with who she was at her core by developing her throughline stories. We tried different prompts but nothing was generating vulnerable or insightful stories. I noticed she was wearing very nice shoes, and I somewhat flippantly said, "Tell me about your favorite pair of shoes."

She thought for a bit and then said, "In the back of my closet I have a pair of blue suede shoes. I haven't worn them in years…." Out poured the story of how she received them as a gift, that when she wore them she felt daring and bold, and that she hadn't felt comfortable wearing them in her most recent job for some reason. "I'm realizing something," she said. "I'm a blue suede shoes kind of person. I value boldness and breaking out of the pack."

A seemingly inconsequential story about a pair of shoes allowed Cara to reconnect with who she had always been and where her talents could shine—especially important because she led innovative technology teams! We kept digging for stories, big and small, that offered important reminders of who she was at her core, and that's how we got her back on the path, step by step, to feeling herself again and living as her whole self again. A couple of months later, she used the blue suede shoes in a speech about the unexpected tools we have in the back of our closet that we need to break out once in a while to boost our energy, our creativity, and our innovation.

Marshall Ganz, my storyteller hero, specifically studies the power of public narratives, or the stories we tell to influence others and garner their support. He focuses on leaders of big movements, big change, but I think we can apply his work to anything we're trying to accomplish by being leaders in our own lives. He teaches that we need just three stories to unite and inspire: the Story of Self, the Story of Us, and the Story of Now.

In this chapter, I'm going to focus on helping you craft the Story of Self. In Chapter 10, we'll look at how to leverage the Story of Us to work on believability as a team. In Chapter 12, I'm going to turn to the Story of Now, an approach to bridging your future story with the present and encouraging people to take action.

The Story of Self is all about communicating who you are, important choices you've made or hurdles you've overcome, and as I mentioned before, the values or character beliefs that have guided you along the way. When I ask somebody for a story to illustrate their Power Words, I usually get an explanation of what their words *mean*. It's great that they can communicate that, but it won't complete the job of being more believable. Remember, it's not the words or phrases you chose that grow your power and impact, but the *behaviors* that bring those words and phrases to life in whatever role you're playing. Story is the best way to share how you've done that in the past, by being fully you, in a way that grows people's belief in your ability to do it again in the future.

It can take courage, but the results are worth it.

Everyday Stories That Reveal Something Important

One day about six weeks after my daughter was born, I got a call that would transform life as I knew it. One of my best friends had died from a sudden cardiac event. She was an otherwise healthy thirty-five-year-old mom of two.

A few close friends and I did everything we could to support her family as they processed the loss, especially helping with her funeral. The moment by moment stories of the days after her death were emotional, deeply meaningful, and sometimes…absurdly funny. A few weeks after the funeral I shared one of them with my friend Caleen Sinnette Jennings, an award-winning playwright who led the theater department at American University. As we were leaving for the funeral, I realized that I would be away from my new baby for hours and that I should pump breast milk. Otherwise, I might humiliatingly and inappropriately leak on people as I hugged them. So I grabbed the pump and we left. In the car, I discovered that the breast pump came with a charger that could plug into the cigarette lighter (cars still had those back then). I thought the idea of switching back and forth between lighting a cigarette and pumping breast milk was completely hilarious. But I was grateful it existed because I used it to pump breast milk on my way to my best friend's funeral.

As Caleen and I laughed and cried over the story, she said, "Now that's a scene from a story I'd like to tell." A spark was struck and grew into a collaboration that yielded the comedic play, *Pumping Josey: Life and Death in Suburbia*, which I performed as a one-woman show, premiering at the Horizons Theater, the oldest women's theater in the country before it closed in 2015.

I thought the story of the breast pump was just a throwaway story, not important beyond a quirky anecdote between friends that captured the absurdity of life sometimes. But even small stories inside or between the big ones are worthy of our attention. And that's why *it's important to start collecting all the stories you can to believably tell the big, wonderful, important story of who you are and where you're headed.*

I get that none of us wants to be "that" person—the one who monologues at the beginning of every meeting with every mundane, inconsequential, and uninteresting story of their life from the past week. One way to get over this fear is to mine your life for everyday stories that actually reveal something interesting about who you are and would make a difference for those who would hear it. They might be small stories from your past or more current stories that offer insights into where you are on the journey toward your vision.

I want you to get in the habit of mining for these stories so you can build your backstory muscle. Let's start with something simple.

The Object Exercise

Pick up an object from your desk or bookshelf and hold it in your hand. Spend a couple of minutes remembering why you have it displayed, who gave it to you and why, or maybe what was happening in your life when you got it. What does that story reveal about you—what matters to you, who matters to you, details about your life that you may not often talk about?

Now, the next time somebody comes into your office or the next time you want or need to build a connection with somebody on a virtual meeting, pick up the object and try sharing the story. Observe their reaction, how they seem to respond to you, and how you feel about them. (Fair warning, I've never seen more people in a room cry than when I ask groups to do this exercise together.)

Big Stories that Illuminate Your Power Words

For Jana Jones and the Saudi CEO and Cara, central themes in their stories helped bring their Power Words to life in their own minds and in the minds of their audiences. For Jana and the CEO, their backstories accomplished something else that was equally important. They offered proof that they had overcome obstacles in the past to achieve their visions. Given what was coming for both of them—new obstacles and challenges—building people's trust in their ability to do the same in the future was super important.

Dan McAdams is a psychologist who has spent most of his academic career studying narrative psychology, or how we use story to shape our sense of self and impact our thoughts about our lives now and in the future—in the same way that actors use narrative to shape how they portray a character. I've adapted a tool he uses, called the Life Story Interview, to help you focus on stories that might reveal your Power Words.[52] (His research supports the story-based approach to thinking about the future we used in the last chapter, too.)

Pivotal Stories That Reveal Who You Are

- Sit quietly with your Power Words and Power Drivers on a paper in front of you.

- Now think about your whole life up to now as if it were a movie. Imagine the important, transformational scenes from that movie, moments when something impactful happened to you or where you accomplished something big. Consider these prompts:

  o One of the best moments in your life and how you responded to it.

  o A time when you achieved a big, big goal and how you got there.

  o A time when you failed and recovered.

  o The hardest thing you've ever had to do in your personal or professional life.

> o   A pivot point for you, or a moment when you made a change and grew.
>
> o   An important lesson learned from a family member, friend, or mentor that changed how you saw things.
>
> o   A time when you applied that lesson, or a moment when you displayed wisdom.
>
> - Now, take your list of major scenes and consider how your Power Words or Drivers show up in them or act as themes running through them.
>
> - Finally, choose two and write them as you see them in your head, as a full, visual, visceral, emotional, detailed story.

You Get to Choose What You Share

One of the oddest things I've ever heard from a workshop participant was, "Ugh, you're not going to have us walking around talking about our cancer all day, are you?"

"I'm…not sure what you mean?"

"We had a guy in who did a workshop about storytelling in sales and he wanted us to start sharing more personal stories and suddenly we're all walking around talking about our cancer and stuff."

Listen, you don't have to talk about your "cancer and stuff" if you don't want to. I know some of the stories I've shared about other people's choices—and yes, at least one story was in fact about cancer—required a certain level of vulnerability. You don't have to go that far if you aren't comfortable or if it doesn't feel appropriate. You can choose which stories to share. You can choose which details to include in those stories.

All that matters is that you're telling engaging stories that help people understand who you are, where you're going, and why, in a way that builds your believability. Are you developing a clear throughline for your character with the stories you're sharing? Find them, craft them, share them out loud. And do it again and again.

In the next chapter, we're going to get into the real work of great story sharing—the out loud kind—no matter what story you choose to share.

CHAPTER 7

THE ART OF INTENTIONAL STORY SHARING

"I get a thrill out of storytelling and investigating humanity from all walks of life. … I never cease to be astonished by the human capability for survival, perseverance, compassion, and love."[53]—RAMI MALEK

I travel all over the world, helping people go to the edge, to push the limits of their leadership, their commitment, their passion. And yet, I'm a big old liar. Because I'm actually incredibly afraid of edges—at least the ones with big drops on the other side. Even bunny slopes on ski mountains scare me.

I was asked to speak in Cape Town, South Africa. As the plane came in for a landing, I saw the incredible mountain that rises high up over the city. It's called Table Mountain, and just looking at it made me nervous. And of course, every person I met from Cape Town would say, "Have you been up the mountain? You've *got* to go up the mountain!"

"Well, I'm pretty busy…"

Now, they weren't asking me to become a mountain climber (although some wacky person suggested I hike the trail that people have actually fallen from). There's a great funicular train that brings you right up to the top and then *slooowly* rotates 360 degrees. It sounded like a torture chamber.

But toward the end of my time there, I found myself speaking in the tallest building in Cape Town. Oh, the irony. I was eye-to-eye with Table Mountain and something mysterious in me said, *I am going to conquer you.* Overcoming my fear of heights and living in a less limited way had been a long-standing dream.

My husband and two kids joined me (dragged me?) on the funicular. I clung to whatever I could reach as we climbed to the top of the mountain. At the top, we could get out and explore. *Well, I've made it this far,* I thought. And then I did the most daring thing I've ever done. I walked slowly to the edge. (My family was right beside me, acting like a metaphorical bungee cord). I inched my way forward. I was screaming and crying, but I did it. Then I fully opened my eyes and saw the beautiful world spread out below me. I raised my arms wide over my head and I felt like I was touching the sky. And my husband snapped one of the best photos of my life.

◦

I often lead my programs by sharing this story. Why? I want my audience to believe that I'm going to take them on a transcendent journey, so I tell a story about a literal one. I want them to feel connected to me, so I'm vulnerable. I want them to begin to see what's possible when we push ourselves beyond what we think is possible. Plus, I love including that photo in my slides. I'm really proud of it.

But what's equally important is *how* I tell the story. It's not enough to know your important stories—stories of the future you're dreaming of and stories from your past that create a throughline to that dream. You need to know how to effectively share them, to build belief in your dream and the aspects of who you are that make that dream possible. Annette Simmons explained it this way. "Story is a reimagined experience, narrated with enough detail and feeling to cause your listeners' imaginations to experience it as real."[54] In essence, it's a narrative that feels real to the teller and the listener. It's that shared reality that helps you generate the commitment and support you need from your listeners to achieve your vision.

Just as beauty is in the eye of the beholder, a well-told story starts with the intention of the storyteller but becomes truly beautiful in the ear and heart of the listener. It's all about the impact on the audience. Research on the power of narrative runs deep. In addition to the oxytocin boost I've already written about, dopamine gets a boost, too, which boosts our ability to remember something accurately, making stories more memorable than facts. We also know that as a person listens to a story, their brain waves begin to synchronize with those of the storyteller—and the more the brain waves are synchronized, the better the listener understands![55] And stories, especially powerful, transportive stories, are more likely to shift our attitudes and behaviors than facts, according to communication expert Melanie Green.[56] What all of this research tells us is that stories are an absolutely essential tool for building our believability with others—because they increase trust, alignment, how memorable we are, and people's positive emotions.

Knowing how powerful stories are for all of us, and we feel it every time we watch a movie that blows us away, why can it feel so hard to tell a story well? I've had lots of people tell me they hold back because they think they're not great storytellers. And I've had the opposite—people who tell me they're great storytellers but actually fall flat when it matters. Unfortunately, very few of us are taught how to construct a story. Most people have a general idea of what a story is, but when they go to tell one, they devolve into data dumps, explanations, or didactic spiels. They rely too heavily on logic and leave out the important emotion. They weave in too many unimportant details and leave out the details that would make the story sing and soar. And too often they don't make it an engaging experience by telling it with expressiveness and energy. (Remember the book reading exercise from Chapter 4?)

All this boils down to one nuance—the vast difference between *telling* stories and *sharing* stories! We *tell* stories when we want to get something off our chest, or we want to download something difficult or something funny. We think it's the right thing to do for us. We've got to get it out, however it comes out, and it has little to do with our audience's needs or wants. These stories can make listeners start glancing at their phones if they go on for very long, like checking the run time for a movie when you're in the middle of it. They're being told, not shared.

Conversely, we *share* stories, especially stories about our visions of the future or the past that make it possible, for the shared benefit of us and our audience. We share stories when we want to influence and engage others, bringing them on a journey and inviting them to dream with us. That's my goal when I tell the Table Mountain story. That's what actors do when they perform for us. And that's what the best speakers and leaders and other influencers do. They're story sharing to engage and connect more deeply with their audience.

When you apply that intention and engagement to both crafting and performing the important stories we identified in the last two chapters, your audience gets so much more than just a flat, one note explanation of what led you to where you are today or of where you're headed or what you think they ought to know about you. They get the engaging nuances that make your character more well-rounded and believable.

Remember, your important stories are like scenes in the script of your life. And if you want them to impact others, you can't read them like you're reading from an instruction manual for your dishwasher. (I've actually had people read manuals *with feeling*.)

Luckily, story sharing is a learnable skill. And in this chapter, I'm going to teach you the essentials.

The Essentials of a Great Story

Do you remember Jana Jones' green journal story from the previous chapter? I believe her story is memorable and helped her connect with and influence wildly different types of audiences for a few foundational reasons. Right from the beginning, it had tension and emotion: her frustration in trying to keep track of her all-important medical notes, not to mention the literal life-and-death stakes of trying to overcome cancer. She shared vivid details: we could imagine her sitting in a patient room, scribbling furiously in her green journal. And it had a victorious ending: she survived and she learned something important about the experiences of patients and doctors. These and other essentials were all woven through, some naturally and some by choice. My story from the start of the chapter is similar, as is, I believe, every other story I've shared in this book.

Great stories need two things: the essentials of good construction and the essentials of good emotional and mental engagement. The first is about the elements, structure, and flow of the story itself, building out the world and the circumstances of the story and, most important, your role in it. The second is about turning that story outward and tailoring it to your specific audience, inviting them into the world you've created to experience the story with you.

Constructing a Story

In *The Perfect Story*, storytelling expert Karen Eber wrote, "It isn't enough to tell a story. The way we construct the story to maximize the brain's attention and engagement directly impacts the experience of the story and the likelihood of achieving the desired outcome."[57] What does that really mean? What are the essential elements of a well-constructed story? Here are the absolute musts of any story worth sharing, if you want to have a shot at moving an audience.

A Main Character to Root For

Every story has a protagonist or hero. In your stories, especially the stories we're talking about in this book, the hero is you, even when it's a story about something not especially heroic, like a time you made a mistake. When we're listening to a story, the brain is looking for ways to process it, relate to it, and apply patterns to it based on our own experiences. So a fully human main character that we can relate to is essential. Sure, some of your stories may seem to be about a teacher or a parent or even an object (like a pair of blue suede shoes), but they are still fundamentally about you or the impact a person, place, or thing had on you. Some of my clients hate telling stories about themselves because they're overly worried about being braggy or getting too personal, but you can't build trust with your audience if you're not willing to generously share with them.

Tension and Progress

Tension is the sandpaper that turns a story into a pearl. It's the exciting question marks that generate a desire for resolution in our brains. It gives us a reason to care, something to hope for. Tension doesn't always require out-and-out conflict (of course, if that's part of your story, it certainly works). What matters is the opportunity for an audience to see the main character striving to overcome an obstacle of some kind. It could be internal, like overcoming a fear of heights, environmental, or human. Even positive tension, like excitement or anticipation, can hold people's attention.

As a result of the tension or the obstacles faced, the main character walks away changed. This isn't always easy for most people because it requires us to describe how we've grown, what we've learned and achieved. But that's the whole point of any story designed to build your believability.

A Beginning, Middle, and End (BME)

Every time my client Emi got up to share a story, the eyerolls would begin and I could see attention drifting away. Her boss told me Emi needed to learn to "land the plane." I didn't fully catch on until she took four, five, or ten minutes to tell a simple story about one of her team's wins. And the point was hard to grasp. She meandered along and then eventually kind of trailed off. Like so many of my clients, I needed to help her embrace the power of BME.

Even a good story, whether it's sixty seconds or sixty minutes long, has a beginning, a middle, and an end. It's why the three-act structure has been taught to screenwriting students for decades. Think about the story that led this chapter. I could share it out loud in about two-and-a-half minutes, but it has a clear BME structure. When a story doesn't have it, we aren't giving the people who are trying to follow along the guideposts or drama they need to keep paying attention, or the sense of resolution and completion their brains crave.

* A good beginning introduces the hero and the obstacle and sets the scene with a few vivid details so that the listener feels they're in the story with the sharer.
* A good middle explores the conflict—internal or external—and progress (see the next section) for our hero. It describes how obstacles are affecting them.
* A good end describes a clear outcome, a resolution for the hero that delivers growth or achievement. What's the result of any action the hero took? What's the satisfying payoff for your listeners?

The great thing about a BME structure is that as soon as you know what you're looking for, it's easy to spot in every story. I helped Emi identify the beginning, middle, and end in two of her stories and asked her to start watching for the structure in the stories she heard or watched. Soon she was "landing the plane" like a pro. For the sake of your listeners, keep the structure clear and tight, with a simple story arc, and resist the urge to take them on a long, meandering flight.

Turning a Basic Story Into an Influential Story

The structural elements or bones of a good story are just the starting point. To develop and share a story that has an impact, put yourself in the audience's shoes and consider what else your story needs to capture their hearts and influence their thinking. Mastering these elements will take you from story teller to story sharer.

Purpose, Takeaways, and Context

Why are you telling *this* story to *this* audience? Or put another way, what's the takeaway you want your audience to get from the story? What do you want them to think, feel, or do? (I'll dig deeper into that "do" question in Chapter 12.) Our stories are more powerful when they're told for a purpose and in a way that aligns with that purpose, so answer these questions before you begin.

Now, flip to your audience's perspective. Your purpose should tie into the context of the moment, or what's happening in the world of your listener right now that makes this a story they need to hear. Think about the CEO from Saudi Arabia from the last chapter who told the story of how his company almost failed, and the hard, *heroic* work he and his partner did to save it. He told that story because the company was facing new obstacles and his employees needed to know that he would find a way through. When your stories meet people where they are now, they'll have a greater impact and build a stronger sense of connection.

Emotion

Emotion in a story builds your connection with listeners. It can be hard to give yourself permission to be emotional in a business setting, but that level of expressiveness can make the difference between a snoozy financial brief and a powerful message that inspires your team. Remember to get specific here, evoking emotions through language that's more nuanced than *happy*, *sad*, or *mad*. Describe how your emotions affect you (if appropriate) and reflect them in your expressiveness as you tell the story.

That said, I once worked with a leadership team on their story sharing skills before a series of all staff meetings to talk about some difficulties the company was experiencing. I sat in on the first couple of meetings and the CEO kept crying—like, really, really crying. As a member of the audience, it didn't feel emotionally honesty or vulnerable. It felt uncomfortable—like he was making the moment about him and his worries instead of meeting the needs of his listeners, especially the need to be reassured. He hadn't processed his own anxiety about what might be coming before getting up in front of his audience of employees. Communicating your emotion isn't the same thing as letting it overwhelm you or letting it become a wave that overwhelms your audience.

The coaching I had done with others on the CEO's leadership team helped them temper their emotions, so when they all showed up together to tell the story of what was happening now and where the company was headed, they reached an emotional equilibrium. You usually won't have others to even out your highs or lows, so think carefully about how you can hit the right emotional tone on your own.

Vivid Details

One of the primary reasons stories are more memorable than facts is because they create a visual image and a sensory experience in the mind of the listener. Great stories draw you and the audience together into the scene, so add sensory detail that activates listeners' brains and ensures your characters aren't stuck floating in some generic white room. The more specific you are in setting the scene for your story, the more immersed your audience will be.

Now, not every detail is the right detail. Look back at the story I told at the start of the chapter. There are a thousand details I could have added, from the color of the meeting room to the smell of the train as we climbed the mountain. But I chose the details that I thought would be most relevant given my purpose in telling the story. This is one of the biggest battles I have with some clients, as I not so gently encourage them to cut out details that are distracting so that the listener can focus on the details that bring the important message alive in their minds. Some people are simply too beholden to details that matter to *them*. Pick and choose your details carefully based on what the audience needs and what you want them to remember.

Try these tests:

* Identify three details for each part of the story—the beginning, middle, and end—that you most want people to remember, based on your purpose in sharing the story.
* For any other detail, ask yourself, What does this really say about me, the situation, the choices I made or the actions I took?

Which brings us to the final point.

Brevity

A story doesn't have to be long to be powerful! And the shorter it is, the easier it will be to remember and even retell. You can accomplish a lot in two to three minutes. The most famous short story ever written—often misattributed to Ernest Hemingway—is emotional, specific, and crushing in just six words. "For sale: baby shoes, never worn." (It's based on a fictional classified ad from the early 1900s.) A much happier brief story is the one I've always told my son about the day he was born. "It was rainy, it hurt, and I *loved* meeting you." That's it. It has emotion, it has sensory detail, and because he doesn't need to hear all the gory details, it was tailored specifically to my audience.

●

Now that you know what any story needs to come alive for a listener, it's time to put the essentials to work for you.

Crafting Your Most Important Stories

- Using the work you did in Chapter 5 to define your vision, write it as a hero's journey from where you are now to where you dream of being in a year, or whatever timeframe you chose.

- Choose two of the stories from your past that you identified in the last chapter that illustrate your Power Words and Power Drivers, or why your vision matters to you and how past experiences will help you get there. Write them as full, compelling, engaging stories that you might share with one person or a group of people.

- Read each story out loud to take advantage of the "saying is believing" effect, the phenomenon that we believe things more when we say them out loud.

Remember, story sharing is the most important tool you can use to connect more deeply with your audience, share who you are, and bridge the believability gap. Craft your stories with care. Let's see what that looks like in action.

Adapting a Story for the Needs
of the Moment

In one of my first sessions with Joseph, the head of technology for a national insurance company, he told me that when he was young and just starting his career, his wife had died suddenly (similar to my best friend). After recovering from the shock, but while still grieving, he had to get back to work so he could provide for their young daughter.

He shared the story without showing any emotion. When I expressed sympathy, he waved it off. Time had healed him, he explained, and now he mostly felt gratitude for his family, who had all pitched in to care for his daughter, allowing him to work hard and rise in his career. I knew that this story could be a powerful way to illustrate his value of resilience and even his ability to be an excellent leader—because of all the skills you develop by raising a child on your own—especially if he infused it with a little genuine emotion. But I could never get him to share it with his team.

Then, years later, I got a call. "I'm ready," he said.

His company was putting on a conference for employees on how to manage through change, at a time when the company was making huge changes in technology and operations. Each leader was required to write a short speech that would illustrate the benefits and knowledge that change delivers, even when it's forced on us. Finally, he saw how the story of his wife's sudden death—the biggest change you can imagine—could make a difference for that audience in that moment.

We got to work shaping his story. We started with the take-aways—the ideas and messages and themes he wanted the audience to remember—and then worked backward to figure out what details were necessary to support them. The first lesson was his choice to change. After his wife's death, Joseph found himself still clinging to the rhythms and habits of his old life, when she was at his side, but that no longer served him or his daughter. So he made a choice to change the way he structured his life, looking at what was working and what wasn't and adjusting based on their new circumstances.

The next lesson was the importance of focusing on the long game. He was spending each day just making the immediate decisions he needed to get through the week. But to find his way to a new life, he had to also start focusing on a new, positive vision of the future. Then he could build a sense of progress and find meaning in the day-to-day.

Finally, he wanted to remind employees to celebrate the small things in everyday moments. As he learned through his own experience, each day is actually a step forward, even when you feel you are running in place. And that's especially true in the midst of big change.

As we developed the story, we considered carefully the details he should share to meet the needs of this audience. For example, we initially included the lesson to let go of what's not serving you, described through the scene of cleaning out his wife's closet. But we decided it wasn't as important in this moment, for this audience. If he were speaking about personal growth, he might have left it in.

Something amazing happened as Joseph began to practice the story with me. All that intentional work in shaping it for the audience and the moment made room for the emotion that had been missing. He now understood the power of using his story to help others, and he felt free to be expressive and emotionally honest—sadness, yes, but also his conviction that learning can come from hardship.

On the day he gave the speech, I couldn't stop checking my phone, waiting for a text about how it went. It came late in the evening because he was so busy fielding congratulations from all the people who shared how much his story resonated with them. Joseph had bridged the believability gap—taking a risk to share a personal, pivotal story in a way that revealed who he was and met the needs of the moment and the audience.

It's as actor LeVar Burton, famed for his role in *Star Trek: Next Generation* and on the seminal children's series *Reading Rainbow,* explained in his MasterClass on storytelling. "We are here to contribute something mighty, and our storytelling is the ship that we sail on."[58] All it takes to sail that ship well, with purpose, is intentional choices. Like Joseph, every time you tell a story, you can make a series of decisions about why and how you're telling it for the given moment. Start by using the questions in the next exercise.

Making a Story Work in the Moment

Choose one of the stories that you've started to craft, maybe from the previous exercise. Now consider a specific moment or situation when you might want to share it to build connection and your own believability.

- What big idea do you want listener(s) to take away from the story? Why are you sharing it with them? Imagine your story has a headline. What is it?

- How does the big idea evolve through the beginning, middle, and end?

- What themes do you want to weave into the story? Or which of your Power Words do you want to shine through?

- What's the bigger context for the story, for you and for your listener(s)? What's this moment all about?

- What details support the big idea, the themes, and tie into the context? What visual are you trying to create for your listener(s)? What details would you include in other moments but could skip for the needs of *this* moment?

- What emotional tone are your trying to strike in the moment? How can you best do that?

Practice to Get to the Magic
of Story Sharing

I used to work for a partner in a law firm who told us the same story about arguing a case before a particularly tough judge every time we were going to be in that same courtroom. Every time. And every time, he told it in *exactly* the same way. We would see it coming and start glancing at each other, trying not to laugh, or mouthing the words to each other as he said them. (I call it story karaoke.)

One day, in the break room, we were debating how many times we had heard it and who could recite it verbatim, and somebody told this great joke.

A man committed murder and went to prison. On his first day, he went to the chow hall for lunch. It was deathly quiet. Every inmate was staring at their tray, shoveling food into their mouth, not talking. He found a seat at the end of a table and followed along, eating silently. All of a sudden, one of the men says, "twenty-three"—and everybody at the table starts laughing hysterically. Then they quiet down and start eating again. A few minutes later, somebody else says, "thirty-six"—and the same thing happens. They're laughing so hard they're crying. They're slapping the table. The laughter eventually dies down again. The new prisoner doesn't know what's going on, or whether laughing along will get him shivved, so he whispers to the guy next to him, "Hey, what's so funny about a number?"

"We've been in here so long and told our best stories so many times, we don't bother anymore. We've just numbered them."

Have you ever found yourself zoning out when your partner tells you *again* about the time they hit the winning home run in high school or when a colleague tells you *again* about that time he saved the day with a client? We've all been there. So, it's understandable that when I ask people to develop a few specific stories to share again and again, they get nervous. None of us wants to bore people with a rote story.

If you tell a story without any thought about why you're telling it now, in this moment, for this audience, it probably will be dull. But consider this: It can take fifty, one hundred, even 150 takes to film a scene. Actors on Broadway might do seven to ten shows a week for months or even years. Actors have to tell the same story believably and with immediacy every time! Every night is opening night for the audience.

You're going to share your important stories, especially your dream or vision of the future, over and over again, for different audiences, in different situations, and for different reasons or with different intent. Every time, you want it to feel as if it's a natural outgrowth of the moment. That's how you make magic happen.

It starts with practice, practice, practice. Some storytellers avoid practicing too much because they worry it will make a story feel canned rather than organic or spontaneous. But here's the truth: Repetition is often the best path to spontaneity. It's how you get over the fear of telling the story and get comfortable bringing your character to life within it. As Mark Twain once said, "I…never could make a good impromptu speech without several hours to prepare it."[59]

Try this intentional practice exercise for one of your important stories.

Story Practice

Choose a story you're crafting based on the exercises I've shared already and do the following:

- Share it with a spouse, partner, or best friend, somebody who knows you well and may already know the story.

- Share it with somebody at work who you've worked with for a while.

- Share it with somebody you just met, who barely knows you.

- Share it with a group of people, maybe your team.

- Each time, do the following:

- Before you share it, decide why you're sharing it with this particular person or group. What's your intent?

- With each telling, focus on mastering or adapting some aspect of the story, like what emotion you're conveying and how, what details you're including, or even how long you take to tell it.

- As you're sharing it, pay attention to their facial expressions and body language. Are they engaged? Are they leaning in? Are they mirroring the emotion of the story?

- After you share it, decide if you need to adjust it. Is there anything you should do differently the next time you share it? Did it work well in one situation or with one group or for one purpose, but not another?

My husband will tell you that I do this constantly. "You're testing material on me, aren't you?" he'll say. Yes. I am. And you can, too. You'll build a repertoire of ways to share a story that allow you to adjust on the fly, based on the needs of the moment.

In my work with groups and teams, I typically make people stand in the front of the room to practice telling their stories…and I film them. None of that makes it easier, but it is great for getting comfortable sharing our stories out loud and assessing how well we're telling them. Give it a shot—literally shoot yourself sharing your own story and see how it makes you feel when you watch it.

When we share a great story with intention, we envelop our audience in our character and in our dream of the future, and we connect our dream to theirs. In that moment of story sharing, we elevate our audience's trust in and commitment to us like nothing else can. Work on intentionally crafting your important stories, decide why and how and when to share them to grow your believability, and then do it over and over again.

PART 3

Grow Beyond Your Believability Derailers

CHAPTER 8

REWRITE YOUR SCRIPT

"While we have the gift of life, it seems to me
the only tragedy is to allow part of us to die—
whether it is our spirit, our creativity, or our
glorious uniqueness."[60]—GILDA RADNER

Matias, who I had been working with for a few months, called to share some great news. His boss was retiring and he was up for a promotion! "Congratulations!" I said. But as we chatted about the opportunity, I started to sense that I was more excited than he was. "Do you have any worries about stepping into the role?" I asked.

He paused before admitting, "I just don't think I can ever do the job like he does it."

"Why would you want to?" I blurted out. (I don't hold back with my clients.)

I've had plenty of bosses who I wouldn't want to emulate, but that wasn't Matias's experience. His boss was amazing—professional, experienced, a people-oriented leader, a creative problem solver—and all Matias could think about in this wonderful moment of career success was how he might fail to live up to that example.

Matias was facing down a believability derailer.

You might be thinking that at this point in the book—now that you've done all the work to figure out the core of your character, your vision and throughline, and how to share your stories—the believability gap should naturally disappear. Hooray! Actually, probably not. So many of my clients hit a wall at this point. They feel like they've done the hard work. Now their behavior should magically align with who they know they are at their core and the needs of the role they're in.

That's when they discover that the biggest derailer to our believability is…our own thinking.

It's exactly when you start to think your character is fully formed that you run into your *believability derailers—inconsistencies in people's thinking that create inconsistencies in their behavior. Those inconsistencies stem from unhelpful, one-dimensional archetypes and the negative scripts they produce.* Yes, we all have baggage and foibles. And no, none of us are going to nail our role every moment. But unchecked archetypes and scripts crowd out what makes us unique and compelling. They convince us to hide, subdue, or to be very different from who we are at our core. They increase our stress and our less effective behaviors. They push us off track from how we want to show up in the world. And bit by bit, they eat away at our believability within ourselves and with others.

And that's the danger Matias was facing, playing through an old script about not being enough that was reinforced by the archetype of his "perfect" boss. It could hold him back from playing his true, wonderful self in a new role, creating a self-fulfilling prophecy.

Growing beyond your believability derailers so you can play you, fully, isn't easy work, but it is important work. If you don't put in the effort to courageously build your self-awareness and acknowledge and address your derailers, you'll never completely close the gap. If you don't traverse it within yourself, you'll struggle to traverse it with others.

So, how do we do that? The work starts in this chapter with building your awareness of the archetypes and scripts that might be directing your behavior, especially those that are pulling you too far off track. Then, we can start to rewrite the scripts by focusing on our ability to grow and leveraging our true strengths, rather than our fears and anxieties, to guide us forward.

Leave the Archetypes to the Bad Playwrights

Bad playwrights and screenwriters tend to create flat, one-dimensional characters, not whole interesting human characters. They default to unoriginal archetypes, which of course aren't engaging, aren't believable. How can a character who is one-note, overly "typical," who never breaks the mold, be believable? And when you're relying on archetypical characters, how can your script be interesting, engaging, uniquely inspiring?!

So many of us fall into the same trap. As we're playing our roles, we fall back on clichéd archetypes or character tropes. We convince ourselves that a "leader" has to control everything, know everything, or force people to comply. A "team player" has to say yes, no matter what. I've fallen into that trap more than once. A "hero" has to sacrifice what they want or who they are for the greater good. And because we have an "ideal" that we're holding ourselves up against—although sometimes it's an anti-ideal—we become convinced we're not up to the role or that we have to live at the whim of other people's expectations. It's the very definition of the internal believability gap—this is me versus this is who I'm supposed to be.

If you've ever read the work of pioneering psychiatrist Carl Jung, you might recognize the term *archetype*. He proposed that our personalities and behaviors are all influenced by the same universal archetypes that define what it means to be human. And that each of us has a dominant archetype that shapes our personality. He also proposed that we all have "shadow archetypes" that drive our negative thinking, emotions, and behaviors. Jung's static list of archetypes aren't necessarily as relevant and helpful today, but the idea behind them—that we are compilations of characters and stories—tends to hold. We just have to be more expansive in how we think about and use them.

I see our archetypes as the foundations of scripts that play out in our heads. The negative archetypes spur negative scripts that tend to get louder when we're stressed, afraid, frustrated, or in conflict. Whether it's a disaster movie-like script about how we'll fail and the bomb that's waiting to go off when we do, or an action-adventure script telling us that it's up to us and only us to save the day, our scripts can derail us. They can hold us back from taking action or responding appropriately. Or they can push us forward, telling us exactly how we should respond, even when it's inauthentic, awkward, or too controlling for our audiences. Can we also have positive archetypes and scripts? Absolutely! And developing or bolstering them (which is what we've been working on throughout the book) is how we can start to override the negative or limiting ones. Because it's our negative scripts that create inner criticism, fear, and anxiety, spawn blame and excuses, and prompt some of our most misaligned and unhelpful behaviors. And they can be self-reinforcing, with one stilted scene or bit of bad dialogue leading to the next.

We typecast ourselves based on our archetypes and scripts. We limit our performance and opportunities to make a powerful impact because we aren't leveraging all aspects of our unique, multidimensional core character in a role. Think about actors like Jason Statham or Joe Pesci or Jennifer Coolidge. They play essentially the same character with almost the same attributes over and over. But now consider the actors who have broken out of their typecasting—and delivered some of the most incredibly powerful performances of their careers. Think Nicolas Cage in *Leaving Las Vegas*, Steve Carell in *Foxcatcher*, and Mary Tyler Moore in *Ordinary People*. Each of these roles earned the actor an Oscar nomination because they revealed the full range of their unique talents.

Unfortunately, just like actors, breaking out of our own typecasting and away from our inner archetypes can be tough. Many of the archetypes we carry around have been with us for a long time, and they can be real blind spots for us. As I mentioned in Chapter 2, Tasha Eurich found that only 10 to 15 percent of the people she studied were truly self aware. But she also found that any of us can do the work to be more aware.

We also may struggle because some of our more destructive archetypes and scripts are best worked through therapeutically. On that note, a big caveat: I'm not a psychologist and I don't play one on TV. This book isn't designed to solve serious mental health challenges that are best handled by working with a trained professional. If you find that you are struggling with what feels like insurmountable anxiety, fear, trauma, or other challenges that are consistently keeping you from feeling fulfilled or happy, day in and day out, please consider seeking out a professional who can offer appropriate strategies, tools, and other work that can help you thrive.

What I do believe, from years of experience both professionally and personally, is that no one knows us better than we know ourselves—that is, when we're being honest and are willing to have a conversation with ourselves, when we accept that we're all imperfect humans and when we understand that it's our job to find ways to grow and improve, we can overcome those internal narratives that hold us back and affect our behavior. Because a key to feeling more fully ourselves across our roles is becoming more aware of how our behavior is deviating from how we want to show up and identifying and ultimately moving beyond the archetypes and scripts driving the believability gap wider.

With any kind of positive growth, awareness of our opportunities is always the first step. So let's start there.

Identify the Archetypes and Scripts Putting Hurdles on Your Path to Believability

Everybody's archetypes are different. They're formed from our unique experiences and the influences in our environments, "lessons" we've learned about what it takes to succeed, how much our contributions are valued, and how to work with others. But in my work as a coach, I see some common archetypes that show up again and again, even if the nuances are different for different people.

I'm always thinking about life—inner and outer—as a story, and so I naturally began to think about our internal archetypes as characters. *I'm not trying to label you or ask you to label yourself. And in your self-exploration, I don't want you to limit yourself to the archetypes I'm going to describe here. I'm just asking you to think about your own potential archetype as a character that might be influencing how you think and behave.* In fact, I think that's the best way to identify them—by looking carefully at your thinking and behavior.

So let's start there, with some of the most common limiting behaviors and thought patterns I see in my work. They're so common, in fact, that I've started naming them based on classic character tropes and roles. As you read through the descriptions and the stories I'll share next, ask yourself whether you can relate to them or whether you recognize them in others. And start to consider how you would describe your archetype.

- ★ The Hero: A constant martyr for the collective good—who comes across as controlling and becomes overburdened and burns out. My favorite hero was the client I nicknamed "Mighty Mouse." He would swoop into a situation, stand with his fists on his hips, and say, "Here I am to save the day." Literally.

- ★ The Stage Hog: The only way to shine is to steal the spotlight from others—relationships be damned. I once worked with a group that was presenting together and the literal stage hog on the team kept interrupting the others in the middle of their portions of the presentation.

★ The Rebel: Defy authority! Break the rules! Down with "them"! All for the sake of the rebel's own principles—whether it's always what's best for the team or not. The rebel is the perennial provocateur, never accepting a decision and always working behind the scenes to upend strategies and plans from on high.

★ The Extra: A seat filler who doesn't go beyond basic expectations because they don't believe they're an important contributor to the success of the team—even though they definitely could be! Like my client who never ever spoke up at meetings. "What do I have to add?" they said.

★ The Jester: The class clown who grew up to be the person who doesn't seem to take anything seriously—and who others can't seem to take seriously. They use humor to mask tragedy. Often, they're so self-deprecating, they tear down their own believability. Humor is one of my character beliefs, but I know it isn't always the best way to deal with stress or conflict.

To help you understand how archetypes can show up in your life, what they look like and feel like, let's look at a few in action, beginning with my own.

The Problem Solver

A few years ago, my most problematic archetype reared up in a big way. I had been hired to help a client develop their first full-day companywide meeting. It would be delivered in person and virtually. I would speak, but I would also coach three other leaders on short speeches they would give, and advise the team on creating an engaging and exciting employee experience.

So when I picked up the phone and one of the organizers started yelling at me about failing to tell them that a virtual conference vendor I had recommended had to start setting up three hours before the start of the event—"We don't have the venue that early!"—I was confused. But I also started to panic. What had I missed? How had I screwed up? And more importantly, how do I solve this for them?

Because that's my archetype—The Problem Solver. This is a big one for a lot of people, especially leaders. It can be tough to spot as a hurdle to our believability because problem solving is a valuable goal or skill to have. And in fiction, problem solvers save the day. Without them, bad guys would get away with their crimes and crises wouldn't be averted. Think famous detectives and brilliant scientists. But in real human beings, this archetype can lead to scripts about perfectionism—because perfectionism is partly about unrealistically trying to avoid or solve every *single* problem, big or small. And it leads to scripts about how capable other people are of solving problems, which can lead to controlling behaviors.

How does this archetype derail me? Well, over the six weeks I worked on the event, my life was hell. Instead of being generous with myself—one of my character beliefs—I beat myself up for not anticipating problems or solving them fast enough. I was so anxious about getting it right for my client and the employees that would be at the event, I took on a list of tasks that were way beyond what I had signed up to do. I was there as a speaker, advisor, and coach, but what they wanted or needed was a logistical coordinator. Instead of calmly and professionally explaining why this wasn't my role and setting appropriate boundaries, I scrambled to solve every problem and felt full of self-doubt when new ones cropped up.

Unfortunately, it was only after the event was over that I could step back and see what I had done. Even though I know about this archetype and the scripts that can drive my behavior, I fell into the pattern.

Why does awareness matter if we're still susceptible? Because I was aware, I could recover my belief in my unique value much faster. I could also better understand my role in the situation and develop better tools going forward. I overrode the script telling me that I had failed with a more accurate script that the event had been a big success, I had played a role in that, and the problems the client was dealing with had never been mine to solve. Then I created some go-to language that I would use with clients in the future—another helpful script—about the parameters of my role in different kinds of work that I do.

Outside of this experience, I'm usually good at spotting when my problem solver archetype is starting to become the *source* of problems and then halting the script by telling myself something as simple as, "This isn't my problem to solve" or "He's perfectly capable." It helps me be honest with myself and others, and acknowledging it boosts my relationships and my believability. And that's really the power of awareness.

The Understudy

Matias, from the start of the chapter, was positioning himself squarely in the shadow of his former boss. He was the understudy, and an understudy's job is to perform the role exactly the way the star does. (Truly, that's what's expected of an understudy. I've been an understudy twice and it's just about the hardest thing I ever had to do as an actor.) Because he had such a specific "ideal" that he was holding himself to, it was easy to believe that he wasn't up to playing the role and that he wouldn't be able to meet other people's expectations. Why should he think that who he was at his core could be a good fit when who his boss was at his core seemed like such a perfect fit?

Hello, imposter, my old friend…

Imposter syndrome—self-doubt about our skills, our competence, our capabilities, even our intelligence—is one of the big signs that we're dealing with an idealized archetype. Feeling like an imposter happens to 70 or 80 percent of all people at some point in their lives, depending on what study you look at, making them believe that they don't have what it takes to succeed in a role, even though other people thought they could shine in it. It's the script that I hear repeated the most. Of course, the understudy isn't the only archetype that leads to imposter syndrome, but it's one of the big contributors.

The Bad Guy

Unlike Matias, who worried he wasn't enough like his predecessor, John wanted to burn down the house built by his predecessor. Where his predecessor had been focused on empowering people to grow, John was critical. Where his predecessor involved people in decisions, John was directive, authoritative, a micromanager. I felt for him. If my Problem Solver archetype wasn't balanced by a deep belief in connectedness, I could have been John.

Believe it or not, John didn't realize his behavior was turning people off and wearing them down. He was shocked to receive the negative feedback. "But that's not really me," he protested. "I'm not really like that. I just thought that to get everything done I had to yell." *Really?* I thought. *Yelling instead of inspiring them, coaching them, or developing them?*

His archetype was the Bad Guy. I'm using the phrase here as a reference to archetypal bad guys in scripts who use intimidation to get their way, not because it's only guys who can carry this archetype. I've known women who carry the Bad Guy archetype, although its generally even more harmful to their professional reputation than it is to men. Research over decades has shown that women face likeability bias. When they're direct or authoritative, or when they break away from gendered expectations to be warm and smile, they're labeled as less likable than men who display the same behaviors. And that damages their connection and believability with others.

The Bad Guy archetype is formed by the idea that we have to be tough with people to make them do what needs to be done. It's stick-over-carrot kind of thinking, and many, many studies have shown it doesn't work. Despite everything we know today about how to build productive relationships and the importance of recognizing people's need for autonomy, it didn't occur to John to try to build consensus, ask people nicely, or even give them credit for their contributions. All he could see was how right he was and how responsible he was for making sure tasks got completed. He was what Craig Pearce, coauthor of *Shared Leadership 2.0*, and his colleagues call an *accidental dictator*—a smart person who makes smart decisions and so is given more and more responsibility and increasingly believes in the rightness of their own way of doing things.[61] But his archetype was turning him into someone no one wanted to work with. It was showing up everywhere, but especially in his virtual communication where he wasn't being checked by seeing how people were responding in real time.

To his credit, John did seem like a nice guy…when he wasn't frantically trying to get more accomplished. And as we worked together, I could see that his archetype was partially driven by his deep passion for the work his company did, a relentless drive to get things right for their clients, and his unbelievable energy—literally no one could keep up with this Energizer bunny.

The Scapegoat

When I started working with Eliza, who you might remember from Chapter 4 as the person who struggled to use her voice in meetings, her leader told me she took too long to make decisions and even when she did make them, she often changed her mind. As we know, she didn't speak up in meetings, even though her boss was sure she had much to offer, based on her professional experience. Something was holding her back.

Eliza told me that she was an introvert, but eventually, I learned the fuller story. She had spent over a decade working in a family business before she joined her new company. Her former boss was the founder of the company and an overlord with a Bad Guy archetype who made Eliza feel worthless and question her abilities.

After working for this person for many years, Eliza saw herself as a perpetual scapegoat—characters in scripts who take the blame, who play the foil to the hero, who bear the brunt of other character's derision. She had become fearful of stepping into the spotlight, apprehensive about speaking her mind, and unable to use her voice to help the team innovate despite her expertise, skills, and talents.

Identifying Your Archetypes

If you are struggling with self-awareness, figuring out your archetypes might seem like a tough hurdle to clear. But more than likely, as you read about the archetypes I've described, you started thinking about behaviors that you believe are holding you back, default patterns that might be limiting your believability. Maybe a recent situation that you wish you had handled differently came to mind. Or you thought about a behavior that's come up more than once in performance reviews. Or you remembered something your teen shouts at you a couple times a month before they slam their bedroom door. Or maybe you're lucky enough to have a caring truth teller in your life who lets you know when you're not being your best self.

Before you can rewrite your script, you need to become aware of your archetype. This is an important practice because you cannot evolve your character and overcome conflict in your story without first identifying the internal role you're playing and how it's influencing your language, behavior, and overall performance. Understanding our default archetype allows us to align our behavior with who we truly are.

I've heard it said that how we do anything is how we do everything, so your archetype might be showing up in more than one of your roles. I know mine does. So I suspect that you already have an inkling, and if you spend some thoughtful time reflecting on key questions, you'll start to deepen your awareness.

Reflecting on Your Archetypes

Think of a situation recently that you wish you had handled differently, that made you feel uncomfortable or gave you a dip in your confidence, where your behavior didn't feel aligned with who you really are or how you want to show up. Spend some time reflecting on and writing about the following:

- What did you do or not do that you wish you could change?

- What were you feeling that prompted the behavior?

- What were you thinking that prompted the behavior?

- How is the behavior *not* aligned with your Power Words and Power Drivers?

- Who or what were you trying to be in the moment?

- When or where else has the behavior, or something like it, shown up in your life?

- How do you wish you had behaved differently?

- How do you think this behavior impacts other people? How do they interpret it? How does it influence their view of you?

- When or where else do you feel like you're faking it or trying hard to fit in?

  Next, imagine a character who personifies this behavior. Imagine them as a flesh and bones character with a voice. You can even turn to characters from stage, screen, or literature for inspiration. Once you've fully envisioned the character, imagine that they're one of your inner voices, telling you how you "should" behave to succeed, to feel confident, to prove yourself, to get people to listen to you.

  Write out that script, in all of its glory, including how it goes in situations when you're especially uncomfortable or least confident.

The purpose of this exercise is to help you acknowledge the one-dimensional characters potentially living in your head so that you can prompt them to exit stage right—or pull them off with a giant hook. But self-awareness doesn't always come naturally or immediately, and if this exercise didn't produce the insights you'd hoped for, my next best advice is to listen to what others are saying indirectly about or directly to you. Think back to feedback from a colleague, requests from your partner or spouse, jokey comments made about you that seemed to carry a whiff of truth, or a recent performance review or one-on-one with your boss (like Eliza hearing that she "wasn't speaking up enough").

One caveat, before you go off hunting for clues: If you're a woman or a person of color, be cautious with performance reviews. Women receive far more comments on their personality. In one large-scale study, 88 percent of high-performing women received feedback on their personality in reviews compared to 12 percent of high-performing men.[62] It also found that women and people of color receive stereotyped feedback on personality traits, and Black and Hispanic people are far more likely to receive feedback that isn't actionable. So performance reviews can be valuable, but they can also provide slightly skewed information about script-driven behaviors.

Regardless of how you learn more about your archetypes and scripts, the next step is to start rewriting your unhelpful scripts so that your misaligned archetypes start getting pushed off stage.

Be Your Own Script Doctor

Years ago, I had a role in a play written by the famed linguist Deborah Tannen. She had written a beautiful script about taking her father, a survivor of the Holocaust, back to Poland, based on her bestselling memoir. She had also written a separate play about the family dynamic between her, her two sisters, and her father that led up to that trip. I had the nerve-racking job of portraying Deborah in her play.

Right away, I found it challenging to memorize the lines. I had never had that problem before, and I couldn't figure out why it was cropping up now! I tried all my usual methods, but nothing seemed to stick. As we began to do table reads and rehearse, it finally hit me. *I didn't think my character would speak the way the words were written.* The words weren't memorable to me because they weren't believable, at least to me as I worked on bringing a certain character to life on stage. It's what makes writing a play so difficult—translating words that work beautifully in a book or that are genuine to what happened in real life to a character on a stage while trying to connect with and engage a diverse audience quickly and believably.

Even though I know new plays are sometimes being rewritten until moments before the curtain rises on opening night, it took me a while to get up the nerve to say anything. But during a rehearsal, I finally said out loud what you never want to have to say as an actor. "I don't think my character would say that." (Cue alarm bells—an annoying actor who thinks she's a playwright on set.) Even if the conversation had played out the way it was written in real life, my argument was that, for me to be believable to the audience, on a stage, the words of the script had to align with that setting, too—and be believable to a big, diverse audience. Deborah was gracious and open to my note, and while it took analysis and effort to understand the believability derailers in the script, when we finally did, we were able to make my character more powerful and engaging.

Most of us don't have the luxury of turning to amazing collaborative playwrights to fix the challenging scripts we're working with, as Deborah Tannen did for me. But your negative, limiting scripts do need editing, and now that you've started to acknowledge the archetypes driving them, you're in a better position to be your own script doctor.

In the rest of the chapter, I'll offer some strategies and exercises to help. What you'll notice is that they aren't about "fixing" the negative scripts, but on replacing them, overwriting them like a computer file, with positive scripts. That's the better, faster, more empowering path to lasting growth.

Map Your Character Growth Arc

Every powerful, human story, like Matias's, John's and Eliza's, has pivotal moments when the characters have to grow beyond the things that are holding them back. They have to break out of their comfort zone and "flip the script" in order to overcome an inner conflict as they're dealing with external obstacles. They have to align their thinking and behavior with who they fundamentally are so that they can grow into their full potential, usually for positive outcomes.

We call this a *character growth arc*, and it makes for good storytelling for a reason. It mirrors real life! We all have an arc. Along your arc are inflection points or big growth moments that have launched you on to the next big moment. Understanding your arc can be the confidence booster you need to overwrite your negative scripts and move past your limiting archetypes. Which is exactly what Eliza, with the scapegoat archetype, needed.

Together, we talked through some of her most important past achievements, from middle school on. We were mining them for proof of what she was capable of and proof that she had, in the past, changed and grown in order to succeed. She was known for her organizational skills and her ability to get things done—she was super productive and very good at collaborating on big projects. But what she realized after mapping her character growth arc is that she was an artist first, an innovative thinker. And every major achievement had required her to think creatively and innovate until she found the right solution or path forward. The willingness to take a risk and even fail was in her all along, it had just been overwritten by an "it's too dangerous" script after years of being yelled at for every perceived failure.

Eliza slowly began to take risks again, bringing her great, creative ideas to the team—starting with her boss until she found the courage to speak up more in meetings.

In doing this work, I've had people discover all sorts of revealing details about what they're capable of, what they're especially good at, and even some of their sticky derailers. They've told me that the emotions this exercise generates are powerful—surprise, gratitude, pride, and release. And it convinces them that no matter what derailers they're facing in the present moment, they have what it takes to grow beyond them.

Try the following exercise for yourself and see what you discover.

Your Character Growth Arc

Take a piece of paper or open up your journal, let your mind drift back as far as high school, even middle school, and remember some of the standout accomplishments of your life. (Side note: an accomplishment that has something to teach you could be anything from leading a task force at work to living with your parents through the pandemic without stripping naked and fleeing into the woods.) Choose one, and do a deep dive.

- How did you feel about the accomplishment?

- What specific hurdles did you have to overcome to make it possible? Make sure to include the internal hurdles—mindset, belief, self-doubt, and so on—not just the external.

- What skills, knowledge, or abilities did you have to develop on the journey?

- What strengths or talents did you bring to the experience that made it more possible?

- How did it help you achieve more in the future?

- When you succeeded and felt joyous and successful, how did you let go of any archetypes and scripts that might have been holding you back?

Next, choose another four or five of your biggest accomplishments, over time, and do the same analysis. What do you see in your arc? What are the themes that keep repeating? How have you grown? What talents have helped you succeed again and again? What are the consistent internal obstacles you have had to overcome to succeed? Try crafting these points on your arc into a bigger story about what you're capable of and how you've grown.

A Strengths Venn Diagram

When I dug deeper with Matias about his archetype, the understudy to his "perfect" boss, we discovered the specific unhelpful scripts that it was spawning. *I'm too young. I don't have the right degree. I don't know everything I need to know to do the job.* If we didn't do something about it, he would head into his new role with this script playing in his head every day. We needed to focus on his strengths.

We identified the ideal he was comparing himself to (easy enough), we described that character's strengths and traits, and then we overlaid Matias's Power Words and his strengths on to them. His first big revelation was how much he had in common with his boss. Then, like a reverse Venn diagram, we created a list of Matias's strengths that his boss lacked. With a little exploration of what had made him successful in other roles in the past, Matias discovered that he has a superpower—process creation. That might not sound like a superpower, but in the role he was up for, it would be. Over the years, the team's processes hadn't kept up with the advancement in their technology and in their changing products and services.

Matias also recognized that he could leverage this talent for his own growth. He created a spreadsheet of knowledge and skills he felt he needed to develop, prioritized them, and identified the most efficient way to learn them. It can be hard for a creative like me to get excited about a spreadsheet, but Matias's work gave me goosebumps. Then he took the courageous step of sharing it with the people making the final decision about the position. Of course he got it, and he's performing in it so well because he has a positive script reinforcing his internal belief in his ability to succeed.

What I led Matias through was a kind of reframing technique, taking steps to focus on the positive rather than the negative. Instead of focusing on how he is different from his boss and so might fail, we started by focusing on how he and his boss were similar. With a more positive mindset, Matias was able to reflect on his own unique strengths.

There are lots of different kinds of reframing techniques out there for different kinds of life situations, but if you're struggling with imposter syndrome as a result of one of your unhelpful archetypes, the next exercise can help. Research by Gallup, which created the CliftonStrengths assessment based on the decades-long research of Donald Clifton, has found that the more time we spend using our strengths, the less we experience stress, worry, anxiety, anger, and even physical pain. Of people who use their strengths for three hours a day or less, about half feel stressed. But people who use their strengths for more than ten hours a day? Only about a third are stressed.[63]

Remind yourself that you've got talents and strengths that you can leverage that make you uniquely ideal for whatever role you're playing. And then start focusing on them every day.

Focus on Your Strengths—And How You're Uniquely Set Up to Succeed

- Make a list of the strengths you believe are required for the role you are in or that you want to go for.

- If you're consistently comparing yourself to the previous person in your role or to a colleague in a similar role, think about what you admire about them, what others have said about them, what has made them successful overall. Or make a list of the strengths and skills that are defined in the job description or by your leader.

- Finally, make a list of your strengths and skills, what you've heard others say about you, what you love doing, what you have been successful contributing in the past. Consider reaching out to the people in your life for their thoughts on where and how you shine.

- Next, overlay your personal list onto the other lists, creating a kind of Venn diagram that identifies your unique strengths or qualities that can help you succeed in the role.

- Are there skills you need to develop or strengthen to be even more successful? What can you do to develop certain skills, how can you leverage your greatest strengths, and what people could you turn to for support in the role because of their strengths?

Changing the Action Lines

We often think that to change our behavior we have to first change how we think, but sometimes, we have to act our way into a new way of thinking. The research into neuroplasticity has shown that when we stimulate the brain, with intentional thoughts or with experiences, we have an opportunity to create new neural pathways. Those pathways can change our thought processes. Increasingly, researchers are finding it's a way to increase optimism and positivity by introducing more positive experiences.

So one way of overwriting a negative script is to create a new positive script by changing our action lines. An action line in a script is a description of what a character is supposed to do and how—like the line in *The Hunger Games* script, "The Tributes burst from their platforms, racing for the Cornucopia," or in the script for *When Harry Met Sally*, just after the famous lunch scene, "Sally finishes, takes another bit of her sandwich. Smiles innocently."

That seemed like the best place for John to start. We could overwrite his script about how effective and successful he could be by becoming a Bad Guy with new action lines that proved the opposite could be true, which would help him make more progress. Eventually, different action would lead to a different way of thinking. We started with a series of small behavioral changes. First, he had to wait at least two hours after writing any email before he sent it. The first thing he discovered is that people often course corrected on their own, without any patronizing instructions from him. And he learned to turn down the tone in his emails. Over time, he started to get a different kind of response to them, which reinforced the new behaviors. I also gave him specific parameters about texting people on his team. He wasn't allowed to text requests (or demands), only follow up communication or information. If he had a request, he had to call or go see them in person. Of course, his requests had a better tone behind them and that small change shifted how they responded, reinforcing the idea that a different behavior could be effective.

Small changes can create compounding changes in a script and reinforce better alignment of our behavior with who we are at our core. Take a few minutes to think about how to replace your derailing behaviors with actions that could help you rewrite your scripts.

Change Your Behaviors, Change Your Scripts

- What are two or three behaviors related to your archetype that you think are getting in the way of your believability? They can be big or small.

- What are new behaviors you could establish as habits to replace them—behaviors that are specifically aligned with your Power Words and Power Drivers?

Journaling!

As you can probably tell from the exercises I've given you already in this chapter (and in every other chapter!) I'm a firm believer in journaling, which is why every new client I work with gets a blank journal. The science and data prove the deep benefits of giving yourself an opportunity to reflect, to capture what you're learning. Research has shown that expressive writing can help us process difficult emotions and experiences and discover insights that were locked in our own minds, especially when we go into it with some direction.[64] It can improve our discipline, our problem solving abilities, and our creative thinking.

Being reflective is an important first step to growth and moving beyond your derailers, but putting your thoughts down on paper (yes, real paper) shifts how you process what you're thinking and feeling. And you can track your journey—what you've learned and how you've changed. You could turn any of the prompts I've given you into a regular journaling practice to spot where and when your less helpful, positive, or aligned archetypes and scripts are directing your behavior, and how to overwrite them. To simplify it, try this approach.

Quick and Powerful Daily and Weekly Journaling

1. Once a day, journal on this question: How did I handle a difficult, fraught, or sticky situation today that felt effective and aligned with who I am at my core?

2. Weekly, journal on these questions:
   o What was a situation that I wish I had handled differently?

   o How did I behave? What was I thinking and feeling?

   o What worked in the moment? What didn't?

   o What would I do differently?

·

When our believability derailers go unchecked, we show up as our default archetype, a shadow of our true selves. These false and less than fully realized characters hold us back from true collaboration, connection, and creativity. When we challenge ourselves to become aware of them, work through them, rewrite the scripts they generate and create new actions that help us grow beyond them, we make room in the spotlight for our own personality, passion, and vision. And that's how we close the believability gap through our day-to-day behaviors and choices.

CHAPTER 9

REHEARSE "YOU"

"Rehearsal is so helpful because…you
gotta push some things away to find what's
underneath."[65]—Taylor Russell

Noelle was a finance manager who was moving quickly up the corporate ladder. Despite her success and clear confidence, she was getting feedback that her interpersonal relationships were lagging behind her other abilities, and that's a problem for somebody who is rising into leadership positions. "She doesn't open up with me," her boss said, "and she doesn't seem willing to get to know her colleagues beyond their roles or outside the conference room."

When I asked Noelle why she thought she was getting this kind of feedback, she brushed it off with, "Oh, I'm not one for small talk." But her unwillingness to engage was becoming a big obstacle for her. It was derailing her believability as she became a more senior member of the team.

Noelle and her colleagues might have named her archetype the Silent Observer—the character who might be full of wisdom or knowledge but chooses to remain mysterious, like the Ancient One in *Doctor Strange*. Outside of work, though, Noelle maintained deep relationships with her family. She was a single mother, working hard to raise her daughter while also moving ahead in her career, and she spent a lot of her energy and time being available to her siblings and large extended family. She chose *responsible* as her core defining word, and that certainly showed up in her throughline of family commitment. She also described being incredibly shy growing up, one reason she fell in love with numbers. She was confident in her expertise—which to her meant thinking, not talking—and thought that would be enough to get ahead. Her character beliefs were *integrity*, *connectedness*, and *collaboration*. *Connectedness* was a bit of a surprise.

"I'm deeply connected to my family," she said.

"But not your coworkers? Or friends?"

"Who has time for that? I have family and work!"

"But Noelle, your job is to help senior leaders manage financial risk, right?"

"Yes…"

"So doesn't that mean they, and your colleagues, need to trust you?"

"Yes, but they trust my opinion based on the data and my analysis."

"That's just not enough. In your role, you need to be able to speak truth to leadership about tough topics, to share potential obstacles and ideas for overcoming them. And in that role—in every role frankly—personal trust matters. Because you're closed off with them, they're not fully trusting you. You just need to extend connectedness into your work life, and every part of life."

About that time, she received a coveted invitation to a weekend leadership retreat with the entire executive team, including her boss and representatives from other teams. They would spend two full days together, including small-talk-heavy meals and other events. For Noelle, it was panic-inducing. "What am I supposed to talk about for two days?"

"What you need," I said, "is to rehearse."

My prompt to rehearse "you" may sound strange in a book about being genuine and truthful. But most of us have been suppressing or have been disconnected from aspects of our core selves for so long, rehearsing can help us find our way back to who we are. Even when we know who we want to be and how we want to show up, it can be hard to bring that true, whole person to life in day-to-day circumstances, like trying to build better relationships with your coworkers or leaders or coaching someone on your team, or in big, important moments, like speaking to thousands of people or communicating about a crisis or a big change initiative. Instead of making us stiff, rehearsing can prepare us to respond naturally, truthfully.

That's exactly why actors rehearse. They aren't trying to nail down every aspect of a performance—each tiny inflection or expression or movement. They're working on understanding how to bring their character to life in the given circumstances of a scene, how to fully embody the character, so that in the moment of action, they can respond from a place of truth.

That's the kind of naturalness Noelle needed to develop.

First, we rehearsed together, with a little role playing. I played the CEO and we just made "small talk." "Tell me about yourself," I said. "Do you have children? Where did you work before joining our company? Where are you from?"

She struggled to see how some of the questions were relevant. "Of course they are!" I said. "They say so much about who you are." Her family was from Ghana and I encouraged her to talk with other women leaders about the powerful and courageous women in her family and their role in her community. We practiced how she would share the story of sitting at their feet, listening to them solve problems and mediate disputes together.

"This is fascinating stuff," I said, and I was certain it would be to others. Noelle was still doubtful, so I gave her an assignment to rehearse outside of work. "You mentioned you have parent's night coming up at your daughter's school. I take it you don't know a lot of the other parents?"

"Not really."

"I want you to work on your 'small talk' with them. Try to build a connection with one or two parents, especially in your daughter's favorite classes, and find a way to tell this story. You already have a lot in common as parents, so start there." I call these "Yonkers moments." In the old days, Broadway shows would go to places like Yonkers, New York, to try out material and do script rewrites. "This is a great test run before you get to the big stage," I told Noelle.

When we talked the next week, she said, "Pam! It was so easy!" She had met friendly parents, she had learned about them and they about her, and she had left feeling connected. She was beginning to understand the power of so-called "small talk." And with some continued rehearsal, she left for the leadership retreat feeling much more comfortable and confident.

Just like an actor, *rehearsing can help you consistently show up as your true character in scene after scene after scene, day after day after day.*

Rehearsing grows our understanding of how our character can and should show up in different circumstances, and moves us beyond the archetypes and internal scripts holding us back. Rehearsing helps us anticipate and overcome derailers that can pull us off track in the moment. So, let's dive into some of the best rehearsal techniques in the business to step into ourselves, connect with our audiences, and course correct when we need to.

Stop, Take a Breath, Focus

I'll never forget the day my boss came up to my desk and without saying a word, stuck a Post-it note on it. In big, red letters, she had written, STOP AND TAKE A BREATH. *Aaarrggghhh!* I raged at her…inwardly. What did she expect? I was a young lawyer trying to get ahead. I thought I had to move at the speed of light, to be everywhere, to be on top of or involved in everything. But instead of bolstering my believability in my role, I was showing up like a bull in a China shop, creating my own whirlwind of chaos and increasing the possibility of mistakes.

While her note was frustrating and even a little hurtful in the moment, to this day I'm so thankful for it. It's the piece of feedback that I return to most consistently.

The world moves fast—and feels like it just keeps speeding up. It's tempting to try to keep pace, to keep adding things on, to keep rushing from one thing to the next. But when we move as fast as possible all the time because we think we have to, we never get the time we need to reflect on our behavior in the last moment or to center ourselves mentally and emotionally so that we can intentionally bring our true selves to the next moment.

Given the extensive media coverage over the last few years, most of us are pretty familiar with the proven benefits of mindfulness practices. Even short and simple strategies, like taking a few deep breaths, help us reduce stress and anxiety, improve our emotional regulation, and allows us to be focused and present—all of which allow us to be more intentional in how we overcome our derailers and show up more truthfully. And if you're willing to do a little positive meditation regularly (that's what the visualization exercises I've been giving you are), research says you can expect to have a longer attention span, better memory, and more feelings of loving kindness toward yourself and others. Plus, greater self-awareness![66]

And yet, the surgeon I was working with a few years ago, seemed oblivious. She was brilliant, but I heard that everybody hated working with her. She was always rushed (this seems to be a recurring theme in the surgeons I've worked with), always barking orders at people as she darted from one thing to the next, and always trying to do two or three things at once—which is a scary prospect in an operating room. She was showing up as an automaton rather than a human being. The first time I met her, I completely understood peoples' feelings about her. She was typing away on her computer as we got started, and when this went on for a bit, I asked her to please stop and focus on our conversation. "No," she replied curtly. She continued to work through the whole meeting. The roots of her lack of popularity and her inability to ascend into leadership roles, when the organization really needed her to, were no mystery.

Toward the end of the meeting I said, "Listen, if you want to be a leader, especially a leader who people actually want to work with or for, you have to find a way to slow down, be more present, and take a moment to focus on people rather than the next task." It was the only way for her to be more intentionally herself from moment to moment. Because she was a scientist, I ran through some of the proof points about mindfulness techniques and then gave her just two to try for the next two weeks. I got an email from her boss a week later that they were already noticing an improvement in her demeanor and presence.

In the world of acting, almost every rehearsal begins with some kind of mindfulness work, including techniques for relaxing our bodies, breathing, focusing our minds, moving and stretching. The goal is to prepare ourselves to be present, focused, calm, and ready to bring a character to life, taking on whatever would happen during the next scene. If you want to bring your character fully to the next moment, this is a good way to start your own rehearsal process. The strategies in the next exercise can help you center and calm yourself throughout the day, and especially before important moments when you most want to show up as wholly and truly you.

Be Present and Focused

When we're not present or focused, it's easy to let our derailers run free. With some basic mindfulness techniques, we can be much more intentional in the moment.

- Stop and take a breath. Regularly pause and take three or four deep breaths using the 4-7-8 approach: Breathe in through your nose for four seconds, hold the breath for seven seconds, and breathe out through your mouth for eight seconds. Science has shown that it calms the mind and lowers blood pressure! To deepen your breathing and strengthen your diaphragm, try the exercise I shared in Chapter 4.

- Relax your body. Again, go back to Chapter 4 for a super-effective physical relaxation exercise.

- Calm your mind. Try reflecting on the following questions to be more present and to prepare yourself mentally for key moments:

  o   In whatever is coming up next, what could get in the way of my ability to show up as fully me?

  o   What has me distracted right now? How can I let it go so that I can be present? You can also write a quick list of things that you don't want to forget so that they're not holding your mind hostage.

Start: Develop Your Character
Step by Step

"Practice yourself, for heaven's sake, in little things; and thence proceed to greater."[67] The Greek Stoic philosopher Epictetus wrote that almost 2,000 years ago, and it still holds true, especially for any of us who have lost touch with who we are at our core or are still struggling to understand and connect with that character. We can start in our rehearsals with the little things to eventually feel comfortable bringing our character to life in big, important moments, when we're in the spotlight.

That's where an old friend of mine, Luke, needed to start. His journey to play his true, wonderful self was full of obstacles early in life. He had a difficult upbringing in a tension-filled home. He learned early—and was specifically told by his parents—that love is conditional, and if you don't meet people's conditions, you shouldn't expect to get anything in return. He carried the classic Jester archetype, relying on humor to mitigate conflict—a survival tool from his childhood—and to mask his own lack of self-worth.

But here's the thing about Luke. He and I were both actors— we had taken an acting class together and had auditioned for at least one play together, although we never actually worked in the same production. And the first time I saw him, I noticed how he stood out. He had "it"—that inexplicable thing that makes you just want to be in a person's presence.

Years later, we met up to reconnect. He had left acting and had taken his incredible brain into the world of tech innovation. He had traveled the world with a large company and was now back in the US. But then he told me something a little disheartening. He had lost what he called his "mojo." It had been tamped down or pulled away by bad managers who had crushed his confidence. An old internal script had come back strong, telling him that his critics were probably right. When he heard about my work, he asked if I could help.

We began at the beginning. Luke's history shone through when we began work on his Power Words. He immediately said "funny" for his core defining word. Despite his Jester archetype, funny could be positive. I had seen him bring it to life for the benefit of others again and again. His character beliefs were "collaboration," "excellence," "lack of pretense," and his Why statement was to bring joy to the world. He was struggling at work to feel that joy or to bring his beliefs to life. "I forget what authentic or genuine feels like," he told me. I wondered if he had ever fully and completely connected to his unique core character. He had learned to build his belief muscles as an actor, where you learn how to believe in the characters you play. He just needed to focus on and commit to his own true character.

I wanted to give him a small, achievable way to start bringing his Power Words to life and overwrite any scripts holding him back. "How are you spending your time?" I asked him. We discovered a host of tasks and responsibilities that kept showing up on his plate or calendar that seemed unnecessary or unimportant. And they definitely weren't aligned with the highest value he felt he could offer in his role. His lack of belief in his own character was keeping him from advocating for himself. We began his rehearsal process by practicing saying "no" from his core—focusing on what he was saying "yes" to rather than what he was saying "no" to. He was prioritizing his beliefs and his unique contribution, because it's hard to deliver excellence when you're pulled in a million directions.

Next, we looked at his unconscious commitments, all the things we say "yes" to without thinking about what it will mean in the long term or whether it's aligned with our character or not. Usually, and this was true for Luke, we do it to gain approval, respect, and…love. We assessed exactly where he was devoting his energy and looked at how he could shed commitments that weren't serving his ability to bring his character to life in his role while meeting others' expectations. It required some courageous conversations and not every one went perfectly, but he made steady progress and his confidence grew.

I asked him to start journaling, especially positive, proactive journaling to assess how he showed up believably in big and small ways. Remember the journaling question I shared in the last chapter: How did I handle a fraught or sticky situation today that felt effective and aligned with who I am at my core? It's a confidence builder and highlights how we're overcoming our archetypes and negative scripts.

And finally, I encouraged him to get involved with something outside of work—a hobby or a volunteer opportunity—that was aligned with his values. When we're disconnected from who we are at the core, we can forget how joyful it can be to commit to something that's aligned with our values. And if we're only focused on bringing our character to life in one part of life, it will never feel totally believable to us or to others. We need to rehearse from many angles and in many situations—just like actors do—to cement our character portrayal. Take a painting class, become a mentor, start running or hiking again, return to your garden. Luke decided to return to his love of guitar and find somebody to collaborate with on songwriting.

All of these small efforts compounded to give Luke confidence and encourage him to bring his core character to life each day. A year and a half later, when his company decided to spin off his division, he had the courage and conviction to put himself forward for the CEO role, a long-standing dream of his that he had only recently been able to articulate. And because of the work he had done, he got it and was successful in it.

In her brilliant book, *How to Change*, psychologist Katy Milkman summarized all the research on the importance of steadily developing new ways of behaving. "Habits are like default settings for our behavior.… The more you repeat an action in familiar circumstances and receive some reward (be it praise, relief, pleasure, or cold hard cash), the more habitual and automatic your reactions become in those situations."[68] This is the power of rehearsing. The more you practice bringing who you are to life in the regular circumstances of your days, the more it becomes natural, habitual.

Rehearsal has to start somewhere, though, and it can often start by reconnecting with who you are at your core in one small way that can serve as the first step. Small, step by step efforts compound. In the last chapter, I offered some exercises for rewriting your scripts. Those can be good starting points. But then we have to bring the rehearsal to our daily life in consistent ways to steadily close the believability gap, internally and externally.

Start Somewhere, and Take It Step By Step

1. What's one small step, one new habit you could adopt and rehearse that's highly aligned with how you're trying to show up in the world?

2. What's one frustration or place where you feel stuck, where you could start to bring your core character into focus to make progress?

3. What's one thing keeping you from bringing your Power Words and Power Drivers to life, and what's one small thing you could do to start overcoming that hurdle to being fully, consistently, believably you?

4. What's something you could add to your life, inside or outside of work, that would help you practice a character belief?

The Magic If

All too often in life, when it comes to playing our true selves in a role, we're assessing our success—or lack of it—after the fact. We're looking back on things we wish we'd done differently, feeling regret or confusion. Instead, why not follow the true intention of rehearsal and chart out a new script beforehand?

That's what the Magic If method can help you do. Constantin Stanislavski developed the idea of asking a series of "if" questions to help actors place themselves in a character's situation or circumstances. It's a rehearsal exercise for connecting with their character so they can show up believably in the moment of the scene. For instance, they might ask, "What would I do *if* I were in this situation?" or "How would I respond *if* somebody said that to me?"

You can apply this same technique for rehearsing how you'll bring your own character to life in a given moment or in certain circumstances. It's an especially effective method for tackling tricky situations when you think your derailers could win out by writing a new script before you're in the heat of the moment.

Visualizing How You'll Bring Your Character to Life

- Find the time and space to relax and focus. Now, visualize the kind of situation that usually makes you wish you could run off stage or at least get a do-over, similar to the archetype exercise I shared in the last chapter. It could be a common conflict with a colleague or getting or receiving uncomfortable feedback. Imagine yourself in the heat of it. Tap into the emotions you typically feel. Step outside of yourself and observe. What's your body language like? What's your expression?

- Take a breath and try to spot the derailers in play that are pulling you off course, the script running through your head.

- Now, focus on your Power Words and consider how you would handle the situation if you were acting as if you are the character you've defined with those words—the character of you! What would your character genuinely, truthfully say or do? What tone of voice or body language would your character use?

- Finally, practice out loud, and maybe in front of a mirror. Or even better, ask somebody to play the scene with you, in a kind of improv.

- At the end, journal and assess how you played your role. What was different from how you've responded in real situations in the past? How specifically did you bring your Power Words to life? What did you learn about any unhelpful scripts running through your head and how to break away from them?

- You can use a short, positive form of this exercise, which psychologists call "resource priming," every day. Just before a difficult or stressful decision, meeting, or conversation, do a bit of calming breath work and then spend a couple of minutes thinking about your greatest strengths and your Power Words and how you can leverage them to get to the best possible outcome. When you work to prepare in advance, you're less likely to be pulled off track in the moment.

Find a Good Director

Returning to the stage after thirteen years in a one-woman show was one of the most terrifying things I've ever done. The director had asked me to take the role as Erma Bombeck without an audition—an actor's dream. But that almost made the fear worse.

Eventually, I realized that the only way to move past it was to put my trust in him. He believed I could do it. His direction would be essential to my success. He would be watching every moment to make sure I was believable. This was live theater, so I certainly couldn't watch myself perform or roll back the scene to see where I was off the mark. I would need his perspective, his guidance, his feedback to course correct.

With each rehearsal and after each show, I added his notes to my trusty notebook—I get a fresh one for each role I undertake to make notes about my character, my perspective on what's working and isn't, and especially my director's notes. And I would return to his notes again and again.

I've had coaching clients say, "Could you just follow me around every day and tell me when I'm messing up?" As much as I would love to be there to encourage them to shift their behavior in the moment, I can't. So I suggest they find a trusted advisor in their day-to-day life to act as their "director."

A director is somebody you can ask to hold you accountable to portraying your character fully, and who can spot when you are being derailed and let you know. Great actors seek out this kind of feedback. "You're always a little nervous to give a great person a note," Greta Gerwig once said in an interview. "But the thing is, they're great at *taking* notes. That's why they're great. They want you to direct them. They want a director."[69]

In choosing your director, consider the people who experience you and witness your behavior regularly and who you trust. Even in acting, everyone has a different method—pun intended—to get to the truth of a character. You don't want a director who is going to tell you to behave more like *them*. Choose a director who is self-aware enough to recognize when their reaction is more about their own scripts than helping you build your believability. You want to find someone who can spot when you're being derailed and then give you honest feedback using a shared language.

Once you find them, enlist them as part of your stage crew.

Show that You're Open to Direction— Specific Direction

Very few people in our lives are comfortable giving us feedback, even when they care about us, our growth, and our success. People aren't trained to do it well, they assume we'll get defensive (because most of us do), and they don't know how to launch into that kind of conversation. Even our bosses or leaders aren't always well prepared for the kind of feedback that helps us grow as effective, believable members of the cast—things like our presence, our communication, how well we're building relationships. And as I mentioned in the last chapter, there's a fair amount of bias even when people are giving that type of feedback.

You can make it safe and easier for them, and more effective and insight-generating for you, by asking them to do it and explaining the kind of feedback you're looking for—especially areas where you're trying to overcome archetypes, rewrite scripts, and close your believability gap. In trying to nail my believability as Erma, I needed help with specific believability-building aspects of my portrayal, like capturing the right vocal cadence and pacing, and learning how to iron like a pro (I know!). I asked my director to watch for those elements, in addition to what he was looking for as the artistic visionary of the show.

I urge clients to create an action plan that they give to their leader, so it's clear what they're working on. But if your director is a colleague or another trusted advisor, you can use something as simple as this bit of dialogue:

> I've been reflecting on when I'm most effective
> and when I'm not, and I think I need to work on
> X to be more credible and trusted. I'm working on
> habit Y or communication approach Z. If you see
> that I'm not being consistent in those behaviors, I
> would love for you to tell me. It would really help
> me build my awareness.

Sometimes you need a director for a specific role you play or a very specific behavior you're working on. I suggest that you develop a trusted network of colleagues, or even friends and family, who can be champions *and* honest coaches, depending on the situation.

My editor on this book told me that she realized that one of her default behaviors was being passive aggressive with her family when she was stressed out or disappointed, especially as her kids became teenagers and developed their own challenging behaviors. She didn't want that to be their dynamic, so she said to them, "I recognize that this is an issue for me and I really want to work on it. It comes down to being honest about what I'm thinking and feeling. If you get the sense that what I'm saying doesn't match with what I really think or feel, just say, 'Is that really how you feel about this?' That will be my cue to check my behavior." And it worked.

No matter who your director is, the most important way to show that you're open to their direction and feedback is to listen when they share it and then do something with it! Sometimes our inability to listen and be open to feedback is the biggest obstacle to our believability. I've bristled at notes from directors as an actor plenty of times, especially if I feel like they aren't understanding the choices I made in the moment. But more often than not, their outside perspective and vision opens up new possibilities.

For example, there was a laugh I wasn't getting from a key line at the end of the Erma Bombeck show, and I couldn't figure out why. My director pointed out that I wasn't pausing between two words. "There's no comma there," I said. "Just try it," he said. And he was right—next show, everybody laughed. Even if you aren't sure about your director's feedback, take it in and try it out. You never know what possibilities might present themselves.

Your Best Day

When I perform eight to ten shows a week, I can't replicate every great moment that happened in the last performance. I shouldn't even if I wanted to, because it wouldn't feel fresh and engaging. Instead, I consider the behaviors that prepared me for the performances that felt the most right and true. And that's the "rehearsal" I do on repeat, like most other actors.

You can do the same, based on your best days. Our best days are typically days when we feel most grounded in our core character, most confident, and most like we're bringing our Power Words and Power Drivers to life to accomplish important things and build relationships with the people around us. When rehearsing "you," try to replicate the feelings, behaviors, and mindset that are most consistent on the days when you're showing up fully and truthfully, so you can have more and more "best days." And that consistency will boost your believability.

The Best Day Exercise

- Think of a recent "best day"—a day when you felt confident, comfortable, like you were showing up as your best self and consequently achieving important things.

- What specifically made it a best day for you? How did you feel, and why do you think you felt that way? How were you showing up with or for others? What were the positive results?

- What got you there? How did you start the day prepared? Who were you with and how did that help you feel confident and truthfully, wholly you?

- What can you learn from that day that you can repeat again and again to bring more of your true self to each day?

You won't master every performance in life. None of us do. We face internal blind spots and external obstacles that take us off course from who we would most like to be, fully and truthfully, moment to moment. But when you rehearse you, even when you stumble, you'll know how to recover quickly, and that matters almost as much as getting it right from the start.

And remember, in real life, you have more than ten shows a week over a month or a year to learn how to nail a performance—you have a whole lifetime to keep rehearsing.

CHAPTER 10

BELIEVABILITY WITH YOUR TEAM

"Frankly, good actors are a dime a dozen, but
I want actors that are gonna be part of my
team and collaborative."[70]—Joe Pantoliano

"They don't trust each other."

I hear this about teams and groups and departments and divisions way too often. And I bet if you think carefully about your colleagues, you might feel the same, at least about some of them. Honestly, how much do you trust them? How often do you find yourself working in a silo, competing rather than collaborating? How hard is it to resolve conflicts? How hard is it to show up as your whole self? And how is that hurting your engagement and believability with your team?

Frank, the head of human resources for a large company, was struggling with all of those challenges. His team was responsible for the experience of thousands of employees—and he felt they were actually making it worse! The sub-teams were competitive and too task-oriented. Important projects were getting bogged down by infighting, finger-pointing, or just lousy communication. And it was having an impact on the HR team's relationships and reputation with other departments.

"On the surface, they seem to be working together," Frank told me. "But if you go deeper, you can see all the little silos." Oh, the infamous silo—people and teams acting like they're alone in the spotlight, never considering what they might gain from being generous and appreciative of their fellow cast members. "If we can't fix our culture, how can we make a better culture for the employees?"

This might sound like a leader's problem to solve, but these types of team environments take a big toll on all of us individually, and *we all have the ability to shift a team's culture through our own behavior.* Again and again, I've seen one or two team members ignite culture change by choosing to show up differently. But it does help when behavior change is modeled at the top.

I told Frank that it would be hard to make progress with the team if he wasn't willing to look at his own behavior and how it might be contributing to the problem. Because in my interviews with the team, that's what I had discovered. Frank was a micromanager. He said they were too task-oriented, but they were just trying to churn through items before he could get involved and tell them what they were doing wrong. He said they didn't trust each other, but why should they when he was sending messages that *he* didn't trust them? Frank loved data. He loved processes. He loved showing up professionally and highly competent. All great talents, skills, or values—except when they weren't balanced with Frank's other values of growth and generosity.

"In any relationship, business or personal, somebody has to trust more or trust first to break inertia and build up positive momentum."[71] Leadership and recognition expert David Novak shared that bit of wisdom, and that's where we needed to start with Frank and his team. I kicked off the first team workshop with an exercise that has broken down many walls over the years. I ask people to share a story or personal attributes that complete the sentence, "For you to really understand me, you need to know that…" (More on this exercise in a bit.) Before the meeting, I told Frank that he would go first—and he would need to be vulnerable, honest, and open about what shaped his Power Words and how he shows up every day. Courageously, he shared this story, and we learned the root of his hero archetype.

For you to really understand me, you need to know that when I was young, I was home alone. I woke up when I heard breaking glass and voices. Somebody had broken in, thinking nobody was home, and they were robbing our house. I climbed under my bed and pulled my blanket around me, waiting for the men to find me. I hid there until my parents came home. It was terrifying. To this day, every night I check all the windows and doors in my house and repeatedly check that my children are safe in bed. It formed who I am. It's one reason I double check everything. I have to make sure everything is okay, that it will all work out.

He finished to stunned silence. He had shared something so personal, human, and understandable. You could almost see the bubble of tension encasing the room pop. And for the rest of the day, we were able to keep breaking down walls.

After that meeting, and with more focused work, the silos began to melt away. People started to talk to each other like human beings. They started resolving conflicts instead of shutting up and shutting down. They called on each other for support and collaboration. Openness, respect, and trust became the new operating system. They built a foundation that helped people and the entire team be more believable.

A well-known aphorism in the world of acting is, "Theater is a team sport." Remember, you are not *you* in a vacuum—and neither is any actor. You are you with the people you wish to impact, lead, or serve. It's the difference between being an individual actor standing awkwardly alone on the stage and a well-rehearsed, compelling ensemble making true magic for the audience.

If you're working on being more believable, who are you trying to be more believable for, if not the people you work with day in and day out? Your success, wellbeing, and engagement at work depends on your relationships with them and your ability to connect with and influence them. If they don't believe or trust you,

you'll have a hard time getting their support and cooperation on your big goals. And likewise, if you don't believe them, how can you tap into their unique talents?

In the last two chapters, I focused on how to overcome the archetypes and scripts that often get in the way of us playing our whole, beautiful selves. In this chapter, I'll tackle how to overcome the dynamics in your environment that can reinforce those unhelpful archetypes and scripts, if you're not careful and intentional. Together, we'll explore how to improve trust and collaboration, break down walls, create more fulfilling connections, and build a true collective that can make magic together—so that you can all achieve more than you can on your own.

Bringing Your Whole Self to a Team Makes Everybody More Successful

When I started coaching leaders, I heard about a class at the Darden School of Business at the University of Virginia. During the winter term over the course of a few short weeks, MBA students had to write, perform, and produce a play. The students came in as individuals and left as a team. They learned about ensemble acting techniques, collaborating to shape disparate ideas into a production, making casting decisions together by understanding each person's strengths, and the importance of having a director! As one student said, "We started as a group and ended as a company."[72]

Reading that line now reminds me how wonderful it feels to come together with a great team for a production. One of my best experiences was a production of *Loose Knit* by Theresa Rebeck. It just felt like we all believed in each other. My favorite ritual? Every night all the actors stood in a circle and passed a ball around, from one person to the next, looking each other in the eye as we held it and saying, "I've got your back." We were each committed to being believable to each other and believing in each other, and it made a big difference in our individual and collective performances. It was like the legendary stories you hear about the casts of *The Lord of the Rings* or *Friends* or *Harry Potter*.

Of course, this is the theater we're talking about here, so I've experienced the complete opposite, too. You can imagine the productions where one person was a total diva, and everybody else was just hoping they wouldn't be the subject of that person's wrath on any given day. Or where everybody seemed set on upstaging everybody else. Or where the cast never "gels," and everybody's delivery seems just off the mark. These situations make for the worst kind of team—a frightened, untrusting, or disconnected one that can't deliver or that falls apart in crucial moments because individuals on the team won't deliver. Think about shows that have been cancelled or movies that have flopped or gone way over budget because of behind-the-scenes drama.

I'm betting you've been on a team like that, because most people have. And I hope you've experienced the joy of being part of a great team—the joy of feeling like it's safe to show up as your whole, true self, generously sharing your talents and skills, knowing that your colleagues have your back. Belonging and relatedness are vital psychological needs that can and should be fulfilled at work, supporting our ability to be more believable with and to each other.

So what's at the heart of these kinds of team environments?

Trust and Psychological Safety Feed Believability—and Vice Versa

I'll never forget the night I was performing live onstage in *Erma Bombeck: At Wit's End*, which is a one-woman show, and things went slightly off script. In a pivotal scene, Erma pulls out her iconic typewriter from under the bed and places it on an ironing board, signaling the launch of her writing career. Every night the audience would ooh, audibly, over that typewriter moment. Ramping up to it with my lines, I got down on my hands and knees to look under the bed and…the typewriter wasn't there.

The show could literally not go on without the typewriter. I started improvising: "Those darn kids, hiding my typewriter," I said while looking around the stage. But I knew I wasn't alone, that backstage, the production assistant was trying to solve the problem just as I was. (She also happened to be the person responsible for putting the typewriter under the bed every night.) As I took my "search" offstage, there she was, holding the typewriter, mouthing, "Sorry," tears in her eyes. I gave her a quick hug and went back onstage to cheers, put the typewriter on the ironing board, and picked up right where I left off. Yes, it was her job to place it under the bed, but it was also my job to check that it was there. We failed together and then we fixed it together. The typewriter was in place every night thereafter—together we made sure of it.

These kinds of moments, big and small, happen on teams every day, sometimes multiple times a day—because we're all human and we all make mistakes. And for anything big or important to happen, we have to take risks that might lead to mistakes. Amy Edmondson, leadership and team performance expert and author of *The Fearless Organization*, found something surprising in her research—high-performing, psychologically safe teams make more mistakes.[73] The members believe in each other enough and support each other enough that they're willing to admit their mistakes—out loud—and learn from them. How we handle them individually and collectively either boosts our believability or limits it, and either contributes to a trusting, psychologically safe environment or erodes it.

Trust and psychological safety are the foundations for great collaboration, professional camaraderie, and high performance because they support transparency, vulnerability, and appropriate risk-taking. They make us more adaptable because they improve the speed and quality of our decision making.

They're also totally interdependent with believability. Why would you trust somebody you don't fundamentally believe, or believe somebody you don't trust—whose motives and goals you don't understand, who seems to be holding back, who wreaks emotional havoc in their wake, or whose behavior doesn't align with who they say they are? If there are a lot of those behaviors on a team, why would you feel safe behaving any differently? If you don't feel safe being vulnerable or speaking up, you'll hold back parts of yourself (like the problem of "covering" I wrote about in Chapter 3), making you even less believable—and creating a giant believability gap for the whole team.

You can see the trust and psychological safety play out in the behaviors in great teams. For instance, another surprising finding about high performing teams is that they aren't all rah, rah, sunshine and rainbows. Yes, they share positive emotions and enthusiasm more than lower performing teams (including more exclamation points in emails!), but they also share *negative* opinions and emotions more openly and more often with each other.[74] When it's appropriate and constructive, expressing our full range of true emotions with our teammates, transparently, allows us to bond, boosts trust, and makes us more believable.

Working on our believability is how we can help our teams do all the things that trusting, psychologically safe teams do—make mistakes and fix them, disagree, point out problems, give and receive feedback, ask difficult questions, take smart risks, and commit. It's no surprise that Amy Edmondson's research has shown that psychological safety leads to better decisions, less stress and burnout, and better decisions. That last one is so important because of the ever-increasing pace of business. We're called on to make split second decisions every day, and the weight of those decisions, good or bad, accumulates.

But sometimes, it takes a brave soul to take the risk of being the first to try for something better. But I believe everybody has the capacity to be a leader in their role and in their life. Everybody can make a positive impact. The question is, how do you do it? How can you as an individual break down walls and contribute to a better team environment and culture? That's what we'll explore in the rest of the chapter.

Bonding with Your
Fellow Cast and Crew

I was called in to work with a large leadership team. When I met with the CEO, Julia, I asked what she wanted to accomplish. "I'd like them to have one [expletive deleted] meeting without me." And as I started interviewing other members of the team, I understood her frustration.

They all talked on and on about Julia, in glowing terms. And I agreed. She was great—smart, decisive, direct, but also generous in her praise and supportive of people. Of course they all loved her. But they weren't playing well with others on the team. They never talked about any of their colleagues the way they talked about Julia. I didn't hear any acknowledgement or genuine respect. I did see signs of infighting, unhealthy competition, and blame. And they couldn't make any decision without running to Julia. They couldn't resolve any conflict without pulling her into it. It was the cult of personality, and this guru was exhausted.

I was worried about what our two days together would be like.

In the rest of the chapter, I'm going to walk you through the kinds of exercises I shared with Julia's team, tailored to be done by you. Because here's the thing—a team is a network of one-on-one relationships, even the one you have with yourself. Every one of those relationships makes an impact. And cultures are just the shared beliefs and combined behaviors of the individuals within them. You never know when changing your own behavior could have a big impact on the behaviors of others and the culture as a whole. And even if it doesn't, you'll see big believability benefits from doing what you can to build deeper connections and more positive relationships.

Let's start back at the beginning.

Share Your Power Words

When I start working with teams—even teams that already know each other well—one of the first things we do together is share Power Words. Bonding with someone isn't just knowing how they like their coffee, it's knowing who they are at their core and what's important to them. Sharing your Power Words with the people on your team allows them to understand who they're working with— the whole, interesting character that is you.

In our Power Words and Power Drivers, we communicate what's important to us and what people should expect of us, and consistency in our behavior is a big factor in building trust. Through our Power Words, we often also reveal our strengths. Gallup, in their ongoing research into leveraging our strengths, found that "strengths awareness had twice the influence on a team's performance than the composition of a team's strengths. In other words, it's not which strengths a team has but rather how well teammates know each other's strengths."[75]

If we know each other's Power Words we know who to turn to when we need support in a particular area—like turning to the person who has a character belief of joy in the midst of a morale crisis. We know what to expect of the people we work alongside. And we have a better understanding of how our individual beliefs, behaviors, and goals can contribute to the progress and performance of the team.

That's where I started with Frank's team and it was one of the early exercises with Julia's team. In both cases, I saw looks of surprise from colleagues who had known each other for years but never knew these important truths about each other. And when I asked them to find at least one other person in the room who had a common character belief or something very close, I saw people coming together who would have said they had nothing in common.

If you don't have an opportunity to do this in a team setting (although I highly encourage you to share the exercises in Chapter 2 with the people on your team), try these ideas.

Sharing Who You Are

- Post your Power Words and Power Drivers in your office, cubicle, or on your desk where everybody can easily see them.

- Share a story you developed about your core defining word in Part 2 with key members of your team, especially anybody you're trying to build a better relationship with.

- Work your character beliefs into your explanations of why you made certain decisions or hold certain opinions, like, "I value taking responsibility, so I think it's important that we quickly fix the glitch in our system that immediately sends all of our customers photos to everybody in their contact list."

- Try the "To truly understand me, you should know…" prompt. I mentioned it in the story of Frank at the start of the chapter. If you're trying to help people understand something vital about you that could impact the team, this is a fast way to do it. If you wanted somebody to really understand you, what's one of the most important things for them to know—beyond or behind your Power Words? Remember, vulnerable stories where we open our hearts to our colleagues are a fast path to breaking down walls and building up trust.

Make the Effort to Connect and Understand

We're all so busy and so caught up in our own needs and task lists, it can be hard to step back and do a little perspective taking about other people's goals, challenges, responsibilities, and dreams. Or even just make the time to improve our connection. That was definitely true on Julia's team.

During my interviews, anytime I heard somebody start to complain about another team member, I would say, "Huh, why do you think they do that? What goal are they trying to achieve?" Eighty percent of the time, they couldn't give me a real answer. They had a high-level sense of each other's targets and challenges—because they were posted or discussed in meetings. But they often didn't understand the deeper details or the personal motivations. Really, their relationships with each other were shallow, and that wasn't improving matters.

Feeling more comfortable being ourselves on a team, and helping others feel the same way, sometimes has to start with the basic elements of relationship building. Remember Noelle from the previous chapter, who couldn't make time or overcome her nervousness enough for basic get-to-know-you conversations? Of course that was hurting her relationships and her believability. Try to practice these four essentials of positive relationship building—based on the research of trust, neuroscience, and leadership experts[76]—every day.

The Daily Four of Relationship Building

- Spend time with your colleagues talking about non-work topics. The more time we spend with people, the more trust tends to increase. And getting to know people better on a personal level builds understanding, compassion, and connectivity.

- Go beyond surface small talk—like a quick "How's it going?" while passing them in the hall or when coming into the virtual room. Deeper conversations about meaningful topics increase our sense of connection faster. Try asking somebody about a story they've shared or something you learned about their Power Words. And listen intentionally to their answer!

- Whenever possible, go to somebody's office or at least pick up the phone to discuss something instead of shooting off an email, especially if it's complicated or a potentially hot button issue. In-person is the best because facing somebody as we talk to them and making eye contact triggers our mirror neurons and boosts personal chemistry and understanding.

- Express gratitude! More on this in the next section.

When I met with Julia's team, after we shared Power Words I had everybody write down what they personally had to accomplish in the next thirty days and a simple statement about why the work really mattered to them. Not the company, *them*. Then, I had them switch cards with the person next to them and everybody had to read their partner's card aloud. What they all gained was perspective and a better understanding that their colleagues were as committed to the success of the team and the company as they were. They were all in it together.

Beyond the basics of relationship building, we need stronger understanding of our colleagues experiences, perspectives, and challenges. You might not be able to do this in a group setting, but you can still make the effort to learn a lot about your teammates. Try this variation on the exercise.

Walk in Their Shoes

Set up a meeting or lunch with somebody you need to work closely with. Tell them you really want to understand their work, their goals, and their challenges better. When you meet, ask questions like these or any others that make sense to you.

- What do you have to accomplish this month?

- What do you love about your job?

- What has been making your job harder lately?

- What fires have you been putting out?

- What's the next big thing you want to accomplish?

If you know their Power Words or Power Drivers, listen for clues as they talk. And finally, consider this question: Now that you know what you know, how will it change your empathy for, respect for, or behavior toward the person?

Show Appreciation for Who People Are

There is nothing like a little appreciation to bridge the believability gap within a team. Focusing on inspiration instead of blocks, strengths instead of gaps, and appreciating what everyone on the team contributes can make a huge difference in mood, relationships and morale. Even our own. Research has shown that when we express gratitude, we feel happier and we have a more positive perspective on our relationship with the other person or feel more connected to them.[77] It also opens the door to allow feedback in.

On Julia's team, no one other than Julia expressed appreciation for what others were bringing to the team. And because of the lack of trust, not one person felt comfortable saying what they needed from others, how others could raise their game, to make the team even better. I decided to take a risk and do an exercise I call Appreciation and Opportunity. Each person stands in front of the room while their colleagues one by one tell them one thing they appreciate and one opportunity they have to make the team better.

You'd be surprised—or maybe not—by which of these is more difficult for people to take in. On Julia's team, the tears flowed more often when someone shared genuine appreciation for something unexpected. It's powerful to hear the positive impact we have on others. And all the appreciation made them more open to hearing opportunities for growth. One team member heard that his wisdom and experience were appreciated—and everybody wanted him to speak up more often. Another heard that she was a great person to brainstorm with, a creative thinker—and the team could make faster progress if she made decisions quicker. And the CEO heard what I already knew. Everybody loved working for her—and she could push back more when she got roped into things.

If you want to show up as more believable and genuine, show appreciation for other people's unique contributions, and see how they reciprocate. Then, you're creating a safe space to have other honest and productive conversations.

Three Essential Ways to
Show Appreciation

- Speak it out loud, and don't wait. The next time you see something or think something, say something. Every day, we feel appreciation for what people offer up, even if it's just a fleeting thought during a meeting—"She had a good idea" or "I respect how he shares opinions without annoying people." And most of the time we never tell them. David Novak, who has written books and created courses all about recognition, and was on the cover of *Forbes* for creating a culture of recognition while CEO of Yum! Brands, encourages people to show appreciation the moment they see something praiseworthy. "Wait, and you risk that person feeling unappreciated for weeks or months. And while they wait, do you think they're going to be super motivated to share their wisdom, knowledge, or good ideas?"[78] Do you think they'll be showing you their true self and full talents?

- Make it personal, fun, and spontaneous when possible. If you want your appreciation to have a lasting impact, consider how you can boost the impact in the moment. Fun, surprising moments give us a boost of joy and stand out in our memories. And the more personal the recognition you give somebody, the more meaningful it will be. When leading KFC, David Novak became known for handing out floppy chickens and $100 bills whenever he was touring restaurants and saw important and praiseworthy behaviors. It may seem silly, but at least one employee asked for his floppy chicken to be included in his casket. I hand out hand carved stones and beaded bracelets with message charms. And I give personalized gifts to each member of the cast and crew on opening nights of plays.

- Write a short letter or email to somebody on your team describing what you appreciate about them or showing gratitude for their support or contributions. I started

> doing this with friends who have made a difference in my life. I save the voicemail message I get when they receive the letter. Hearing their joy in someone taking the time to tell them what they bring to the world... well, that brings me joy.

The first time I went to the headquarters for a new client, I was met by the most wonderful man. He was the facilities manager, and when I walked in, I felt like I was being greeted by a brass band parade. He made me feel so welcome, and he was so helpful, making sure I had absolutely everything I needed for the day-long workshop I would be leading.

As I travelled around the country working with different teams in satellite offices, I asked them to work on expressing appreciation by writing letters to people in the company. And in every group at this organization, at least a couple people said they would write to him. It wasn't just me. He made everybody who came to the company headquarters, no matter their position, feel special and supported.

When I went back for a final event, he showed me his stack of letters with pride and his own brand of humble gratitude.

Getting Past Conflict

In our two days together, Frank's HR team, from the start of the chapter, made a lot of progress. I was proud of them for breaking through barriers, but I knew it wouldn't be enough. Old habits and all that. And as I started one-on-one coaching with key leaders, I found some of the problematic ones.

Olivia told me she was at the end of her rope with one teammate, with the unfortunate name Dick. And trust me, she took *every* opportunity to emphasize that name each time she complained about some frustrating behavior of his. Mostly, it boiled down to the fact that he allowed the members of his team to behave badly toward the members of her team. They were obstructive and unpleasant. When I asked her what she had tried, she said that she had spoken to him about it and he had turned it around on her team and their unreasonable demands. And that was it. She just kept stewing without doing anything more about it. One of her character beliefs was transparency. "Are you being transparent with him?" I asked. "Other than your attitude, does he even know there's a real problem?"

One of the biggest issues that derails teams is unresolved—and often, unacknowledged or unspoken—conflict. Fear of conflict is one of the dysfunctions that leadership expert Patrick Lencioni describes in *The Five Dysfunctions of a Team*, one of the bestselling team performance books of all time. When you're not aligned with another team member, when it's rough and angsty and just not going well, it's not only you who suffers. It makes me think of stage or screen productions that were riddled with "creative differences"—the PR phrase for unresolved conflict that drives people to quit, or worse, stay and make everybody miserable for weeks or months.

To be a successful, believable, member of a team who has a positive influence, the best thing you can learn to do is resolve conflict—early and often. It can be difficult, though, because if our archetypes and scripts show up anywhere, it's in our behavior toward people we're in conflict with. And that makes it even harder to approach the situation as our best, true self. But that doesn't mean it's impossible.

You can use fierce conversations, crucial conversations, radical candor, the next conversation…or any of the other totally valid approaches out there that work for you and the situation. Whatever method you choose, you still have to start at the same place—with you. That's what the next exercise is designed to help with.

Resolving Conflict, Starting with You

If you're in conflict with somebody on your team, even if it's low-level conflict, spend time thinking about or journaling about the following questions.

- How would you describe the core issue? How do you think the other person might describe it?

- What are the basic facts? No opinions or feelings here.

- What's the story you're telling yourself—and maybe others, too—about the other person?

- How does the conflict or the story make you feel? Which archetypes or scripts rear up for you when you think about the conflict or deal with the other person?

- What's the believability gap between the two of you? Does the other person know or get to see the whole, real you?

- What's one thing you could start doing differently that would be aligned with your Power Words and could shift the conflict?

I worked through these questions with Olivia and it revealed that a big source of the conflict was simply a lack of communication—it usually is! "Honestly, the thing I should really be doing is addressing the behaviors as they happen with Dick," she acknowledged, finally saying the name with less snark.

"That would certainly be more transparent," I said. And she set up a meeting with him right then.

We met again two weeks later, and her energy was very different. "You seem lighter," I said.

"It's relief," she said. "Dick handled the conversation well. Things aren't perfect, but he's listening, and he has already addressed a couple of big obstacles with his team. And I'm working on some issues with my team, too. It's a start." And that's the most important thing with conflict resolution—to start.

Improvise Your Way to Better Collaboration

The most important work of any team is collaboration—that beautiful melding of everybody's unique contributions, ideas, and talents to create something so much better than anybody could produce on their own. As director Sam Mendes has said, "You have twenty other imaginations in the room with you as a director, and you're an idiot if you don't use those imaginations. There are some incredibly intelligent people in the room with you who see it with every bit as much insight as you do."[79]

Actors work with this focus every moment, and one way they build good collaboration skills is by practicing improv. Chris Messina, who you might know from *The Mindy Project* and the movie *Air*, where he played Michael Jordan's rep, is known for being an exceptional collaborator—*and* improving his way through some of his greatest scenes. "It's almost exhausting, the level of honesty and truth he brings to every scene," Mindy Kaling once said in an interview.[80]

I don't want you to exhaust your colleagues, but I do want you to be able to respond honestly, truthfully, from your core, in all kinds of situations. And create room for others to do the same. Because that's the root of great, productive, psychologically safe collaboration. And that's all improv really is—bringing who you are to the moment with an open mind to create something amazing together. If we follow the rules of great improvisation, we might learn something about ourselves, our teammates, and the opportunities in front of us. And then we can solve our biggest challenges and achieve our greatest potential.

Practice the Rules of Improvisation

In your next meeting, conversation, and problem-solving huddle, focus on these improv behaviors and see how far they take you in showing up as more you and helping others do the same.

- Say "Yes, and": You have something unique and important to contribute. Do so. Try repeating back what you heard the other person say and then build on it with your point of view.

- Be a great listener: Your teammates have something unique and important to contribute, too. Give them the space and time to do so and consider how your mutual contributions could create something greater. Ask open-ended questions to better understand their ideas and perspectives.

- Come from a place of positivity and have an open mind: Remember, somebody has to extend trust first. Make that person you. Trust in the good intentions of your teammates and your shared goals. Work on using positive, affirmative, trust-building language with others that brings generosity to your interactions, like, "That's a good point" or even simply, "You're right."

- There are no mistakes, just beautiful opportunities: Do your part to create a safe space for failure and recognize when others are doing the same for you. Try acknowledging mistakes you've made or an idea you presented that didn't turn out to be the best one. Try to let go of the need to be "right" and think of every idea is just one more contribution to the next great solution.

The Story of Us:
Develop Shared Stories and Purpose

With Julia's team, I wanted to keep cementing the idea that everybody was committed to their collective success and the mission of the company. I wanted to elevate their sense of communal purpose rather than seeing Julia as the source of all motivation and drive.

One important way we did that was to work on the Story of Us. Remember Marshall Ganz's model of three stories—Story of Self, Story of Us, Story of Now—I described in Chapter 6? The Story of Us "expresses the values and shared experience of the 'us' you want to evoke."[81] It creates a throughline for the team! It highlights challenges, successes, and choices made in key moments that propelled the team forward, making the whole team more believable to its members and to the others outside the team.

It might be a bit harder to do this kind of work on your own, as a team member. If you're a leader, bring the team together to start collecting the kinds of belief- and connection-building stories I've listed next. If you're not a team leader, find ways to start sharing any stories you know of team successes, like the following, and see how people respond.

★ Successes you all contributed to.
★ Moments of impact that make you feel proud.
★ Projects where the team overcame big challenges, together.
★ Moments when one team member came to another's rescue.
★ Above and beyond moments when you offered superlative service or support.

Julia's team came up with some great ones. Like the time the CFO "borrowed" a vacuum cleaner from a cleaning closet at a convention center to clean a dirty rug at the trade show booth an hour before their biggest client was scheduled to appear. I heard that story more than once as I attended company events over the next few months. It quickly became company legend, communicating that everybody rolls up their sleeves to get the job done right, no matter their title.

The stories you find to share may be your own or they may be stories you've heard from others. What matters is that you share them to influence the culture of the team and build your sense of connection by highlighting what you all do well and what you're capable of when you work together. That's what we all want to feel and experience when we're working with others to make important things happen. And in the next part, I'll help you create that same kind of engagement and excitement with the people you most want to influence.

PART 4

Excite Your Audience

CHAPTER 11

BREAK THE FOURTH WALL

"I love the chemistry that can be created
onstage between the actors and the audience.
It's molecular even, the energies that can
go back and forth."[82]—GLENN CLOSE

Some years ago, I was helping organize an event for a couple thousand CEOs from all over the world. We had engaged Wyclef Jean, rapper and founding band member of The Fugees with Lauryn Hill, to perform and share his story of growing up in Haiti. And we had asked him to do it at 10:00 a.m. I believe it's not a great idea for vampires, actors, or musicians to be seen in broad daylight, and early morning isn't a great time to crank the volume and get a senior-level business audience amped up—especially for a musician with Wyclef's schedule. But he didn't bat an eye. Instead, he seemed most interested in making sure that the audience would be engaged by the performance.

On the day of the event, he brought his whole, energetic, rock-star self into the moment—and he got 2,000 CEOs to do the same! He had them out of their seats, dancing with abandon. They even formed a huge conga line around one of the largest ballrooms I've ever seen. I couldn't believe it. If you want to see how he did it, watch the video of him performing at the Nobel Peace Prize concert for President Barack Obama. He achieved that same level of audience engagement and excitement, but this time with kings, princes, and leaders of the free world.

Wyclef is a master of making the members of his audience, no matter who they are, feel like they're the rockstars by pulling them into the moment, into the "performance." He's a master of breaking through the fourth wall. In acting lingo, the "fourth wall" is the conceptual barrier between the audience and the actors and the world they're creating. It's named for the imaginary fourth "wall" of the "room" of a stage. When an actor ignores that barrier and talks directly to the audience—like Matthew Broderick did in *Ferris Beuller's Day Off*, Margo Robbie did in *The Big Short*, and everybody did in *The Office*—they're pulling the audience into the story, making them feel a part of it. When they do it well and powerfully, the audience is fully in the moment, transported into the emotional world of the play or film, and more deeply connected to the character speaking to them.

Ultimately, all the work we do to figure out how to be believable in how we show up is pointless without having someone to show up *for*. I'll say it again: you aren't *you* in a vacuum. You are who you are with and for others. Playing you believably is just as much about how you make your audience feel and think in the moment—whether that's one person or one thousand—as it is about understanding your own character. An interviewer once asked actor Christoph Waltz, who won an Academy Award for his role in *Django Unchained*, what makes him interested in a particular role. Waltz's reply was priceless. "That is absolutely irrelevant. The important thing is: What makes the audience interested in it?"[83]

Whether it's a persuasive conversation with a colleague, a regularly weekly meeting, or one of the most important presentations of your life on an actual stage, you have an opportunity to entice people to come on a journey with you or support you in your journey toward your vision. You have an opportunity to create a deep and energizing connection with your audience, which is any person you interact with in a meaningful way. You may or may not want them to get out of their seats and form a conga line, but you definitely want them to be engaged, to interact! Every member of your audience is living in their own world, though, focused on their own needs and challenges, dealing with their own believability gap. Your job is to get them to feel something about themselves, about the importance of their role, and consequently about you, so that you can inspire and influence them. To do that, you have to meet them where they are, make them feel that you understand them, invite them into your story, and convince them to come on a journey with you—to break the metaphorical fourth wall!

All the work you've been doing to figure out who you are and get out of your own way has been vital preparation for building deeper connections with others. It's hard to build a connection between who you fundamentally are and who your audience fundamentally is if you're leaving your most compelling, believable self "off-stage," so you have to start there.

After all the work you've done, now, in this chapter, we can focus on the fundamentals of relational intelligence—understanding your audience and bringing the right energy to all your interactions to create a meaningful connection. It all starts with learning about your audience and then doing the work to make them feel like you own the room together through the energy you bring to the moment. Let's start by exploring what's happening in people's brains when we make the effort to connect.

The Science of Connection

The first time I experienced the full power of deep connection as an audience member, I was just a teenager watching George C. Scott play Willy Loman in *Death of a Salesman*. During one of the final scenes, when Willy has slipped deep into despair and irrationality, I started to sob. I tried to be quiet, especially because it was a theater in the round and the people sitting on the other side of the stage could see me. But when I looked up, I could see they weren't focused on me at all. They were there with Willy, just like I was, because breaking the fourth wall closes the emotional distance.

I'm sure you can immediately think of moments when you were in the audience and felt a powerful connection to the person on stage or screen. Great actors make that happen for us. And our favorite actors really do. Research has shown that fans have a physical and emotional reaction to watching their favorites. But you don't need research to remind you how you feel when you're watching your favorite team, actor, or musician. You get flushed and excited, you're more present, you feel connected to them, as though you belong in their community—something we all long for.[84] In an interview, Academy Award winner Brie Larsen acknowledged how important this is on a basic human level. "What I am looking for in this world is a sense of not feeling alone, and that's one of the greatest gifts you can give to another person. I hope that my work does that. I hope that when people leave the theater, they feel less alone."[85]

Your audience is sitting there just waiting, hoping, to feel connected to you—to feel anything, honestly. They might be looking at you, but they're probably not thinking about you—about whether you're nervous or uninspired or worried about the coffee you spilled on yourself just before they walked into your office. They're thinking about themselves, hoping you will care about them enough to make them feel like they matter. And given that emotions are often more important than facts when we're trying to persuade or influence people, making sure your audience feels something just by being in your presence is critical to building a connection with them.[86]

This is especially important in our modern world where more and more of our interactions and communications are becoming virtual, moving online. We can focus on how these changes are dissipating connection and breaking down confidence, or we can learn that even these interactions that can seem loaded with potential self-serving pitfalls are actually opportunities to build connection and make an impact. New technology and platforms are just new conduits for connection with all our audiences. And if you want be believable you have to be believable both IRL and on any platform.

All of the exercises and reflection I'll describe in this chapter and the next are just as important, if not more so, today because of these changes in how we communicate. The thought leaders with the biggest followings and the strongest connections create content that is focused on others rather than themselves, that is genuine, that is designed to have an impact rather than just add to the noise. They recognize what people want and need, what they're struggling with, whether they need empathy or a kick in the pants to feel inspired, and they reflect all of that in how they bring who they are and their ideas to every interaction, even on their shortest posts or brief videos. Take a look at Adam Grant or Brené Brown on different social platforms to see what this looks like in action. Think about it this way: if more of us show up genuinely and generously online, we could change the impact, deepen the connection, and transform the virtual landscape into one of generous and thoughtful interaction.

As the brilliant psychologist and relationship expert Esther Perel wrote, "Connection is not a transaction; it's a vibrational field we can tap into on a daily basis in the most mundane of circumstances."[87] *Every* interaction we have with our audiences is an opportunity to make them feel seen, understood, and ultimately, moved. It's the basis of relational intelligence—the skill of understanding others, balancing their needs with yours, and building trust with them. And when we develop and use that muscle, the audience's perception of us changes.

Let's begin by getting to know the most important people in the room—your audience.

Get to Know Your Rock Stars

Gabriel, a CFO I was coaching, was struggling with a direct report, Hana, who was responsible for overseeing a big change in software vendors. Hana just would not commit. She couldn't make a decision. Gabriel needed his team leaders to make decisions or he'd be pulled into every one of them and away from his own work. "She's come to me ten different times to discuss the pros and cons!" he said, exasperated. He did not want to be solving people's problems for them. But so far, nothing he had said had budged this particular manager off the fence.

"Do you know why Hana is hesitating, or what she might need from you to feel confident about making the decision?" I asked.

"I've told her I want her to make it."

"But is that what she needs to hear to step into the decision-making spotlight? Because that's what you're asking her to do," I explained. Gabriel hadn't taken the time to get to know his "audience" deeply, this person he was trying to engage, lead, and influence. He wouldn't be able to do any of those things successfully until he did.

Are you struggling right now to build connection or excitement with a person or a team? Or do you feel like when you get on stage, even if that means sharing an idea at a department meeting, you're not having the impact you want? Does it seem hard to get them to really believe in you?

The question I always start with when I hear about these struggles from clients is, how well do you know them? Let's face it—any time we're in the audience, we want whoever is talking to make it about us. We want to know what's in it for us. We want to feel that they're paying attention to our needs. We want that magical moment when they make us feel like we *matter*. And when they do, we believe them more and are more open to hearing what matters to them.

Making people feel like they matter isn't hard to do. Just consider your audience's perspective and answer four simple questions. Gabriel agreed to work through them, giving them serious thought—and it was revelatory.

1. Who is your audience—the people you're trying to impact, lead, or serve—and what do they need and want?

The first part of this question may seem obvious. Of course you know who your audience is. For Gabriel, it was his team, and specifically Hana. Great, but how much did he really understand her?

We move from interaction to interaction every day without giving this question much thought. Who is this person or this group of people I'm talking to? What's their title? What do they actually do day after day? You can even go more granular if it makes sense to do so. What generation are they from? What's their background? What's their expertise? What are they known for? What makes them uniquely *them*? The answer to each of these questions could illuminate not only who they are but also what is important to them.

It's so much easier to build a connection when you start with an understanding of what your audience needs and wants rather than assuming from the start that you want the same things. Try putting yourself in their shoes. Consider their circumstances carefully—what their day or week or year has been like, what they're carrying into the room with them, mentally and emotionally. Now imagine you are the person in the audience and ask yourself—what is on my mind right now, in this moment? What do I want to get out of this?

I've had multiple people say to me over the years, "But I'm just making this up. I'm just imagining what they would say."

"Yes," I say. "That's called empathy and experience." They've probably given you clues in past conversations or in their behavior that are guiding as you're "making up" your answer. Or if you're talking to a big group, it might be based on research and data—if you're talking to a big sales team, you might know that it's been a tough year and the people in the room are desperate for some good news or good ideas. And whenever possible, try asking! I gather all sorts of information about the teams I work with before I meet with them, to understand their challenges, opportunities, and dynamics. What matters most is that you take the time to consider their perspective with intention.

Gabriel knew that Hana needed and wanted his approval. She also wanted to be promoted. Understanding these basic needs could shape how he communicated. He wanted to empower her and get her moving. Instead of taking her step by step through what she should do, he needed to let her shine and gain that much desired approval and success. He decided to set a meeting for Hana to present her plan in detail, giving her an opportunity to build her confidence in her choice and get his support and reassurance. And it put a deadline on the decision.

I often hear, "How can I meet the needs of a large group when they all have different needs?" Of course an audience is made up of individuals, but you can always take the time to research your audience, break them into groups with more distinct needs—people at different levels of an organization, people from different departments, people from different backgrounds or professions, etcetera. Then you can find a way to connect with each of those needs at some point during a meeting, presentation, or speech. Trust me, they'll feel it if you ignore their needs completely and they'll deeply appreciate it when you acknowledge what's on their mind.

2. What's at risk for them if they don't get what they want or need?

We usually know what's at risk for us if we aren't able to influence or persuade our audience. Unfortunately, sometimes it's all we can think about, and that definitely keeps us from being believable with them. Again, try putting yourself in your audience's shoes and ask, what specifically could happen in my work, career, or life if I don't get the things I need out of this moment?

Based on things Hana had said and her behavior, Gabriel realized that his manager was afraid that somebody (him!) would get mad at her for her choice and that her career would be on the line if it didn't work out. Well, sure that's always a risk, but in this case analysis paralysis was leading to the result she was most afraid of. He needed to remind her that her job was about making decisions and moving forward, that it was key to showcasing what she was capable of. And he could also remind her of other successful decisions she had made and programs she had led. Most important, he could reiterate his faith and trust in her.

3. How does what you are trying to accomplish align with their wants and needs?

Tony Award winner Brian Stokes Mitchell once said, "I love when you walk out [of the theater] and realize we're the same and we want the same thing."[88] That's the best outcome of any interaction, right? When you can find a way to align what your audience wants with what you want, so that you can move forward together, you've developed a connection through a shared future.

Given what you know about your audience, consider how you can make that alignment happen. A great starting point is your vision of the future. How does that overlap with their needs and desires? What about the bigger picture vision for the team or community? Remember the Story of Us I described in Chapter 10 and think about how you can weave that into your communication.

Hana's project was just one part of a huge transformation for the whole division of the company. And Gabriel, who was responsible for his team's contribution, knew the rest of the team was depending on the shift in vendor and the new systems that would make the rest of the transformation easier. He needed to get Hana excited about her contribution to the big picture by making this decision, how it would help hundreds of people. He needed to inspire her to be part of the change to override the overwhelming pressure she was feeling.

4. Why are you the right person, right now, to help guide them from where they are to where you all want to be?

In every interaction, we bring something unique to our audience. We have something to offer of value, something beneficial to share. It may be as simple as a supportive presence, somebody to listen and understand. Or it could be deep insights based on our experience. Whatever it is, understanding the value we bring boosts our connection and believability.

A good starting place is your How statement from your Power Drivers. Ask yourself, how would it play out in or influence your efforts to meet your audience's wants and needs?

Gabriel's How statement was, "I am a servant leader who drives growth with directness and integrity." And it captured his relationship with Hana pretty well. He had helped her grow ever since she had started as an intern. He'd guided and mentored her, and he now had an opportunity to help her overcome an internal obstacle by being direct with her. He'd done it in the past and he needed to make it clear that he'd do it again, that she could trust him and herself.

Take the time to answer these questions about your audience and you'll start to understand how to bring your full self, your whole character, into your interactions to excite and engage them. You'll build alignment between your character and theirs and take one more step toward closing the believability gap.

Gabriel used these tools to prepare for his next meeting with Hana. He began the conversation powerfully, addressing everything he now understood about Hana and his opportunity to coach. "I want you to take the risk of choosing the vendor you think is our best option now—and possibly fail. You can't know the future and neither can I, but I trust you to handle it if it doesn't work out. We'll still be better off in the end than we are now, and you'll allow everybody else to move forward, too."

Building the Right Energy to Connect

Getting to know one member of his audience better helped Gabriel uncover a believability gap he had with his team. His core defining word was *integrity* and two of his character beliefs were growth and service. All of that meant that he really wanted—and needed—to empower his team. But when people made decisions that didn't work out....well, he wasn't giving them what they needed to feel empowered the next time. Instead, he almost always asked, "Tell me why you made that decision," which sounded blame-y. Gabriel thought he was encouraging them to be analytical, but they perceived it as criticism or judgment, because he wasn't considering the energy his questions conveyed from him and evoked in others.

He started simply, by clarifying and being intentional about the energy he wanted to convey to his entire team: understanding and encouragement. From there, he changed his approach. For instance, instead of starting off by asking them why they made a particular decision, he asked them what they thought they should do or what they planned to do next. He was showing that he still had confidence in their decision making and problem-solving abilities. If they were struggling, he brainstormed possibilities but left the final decision up to them. Eventually, even the logistics of his meetings changed. Multiple fifteen-minute conversations that disrupted his days turned into twice-monthly, hour-long deep dives with his direct reports, during which he was less distracted and more present for problem-solving, coaching, and celebrating successes.

Gabriel reframed how he was showing up so that he could be there for his audience, fulfill their needs and his, and deepen his connection with them. By shifting his energy to convey generosity, support, and empathy, balanced with accountability, he was more effective at influencing their behavior—because they believed he really did want to empower them.

Actor and singer Cynthia Erivo, of the megahit movie *Wicked* and many award-winning roles on Broadway, described what she's striving for when she's on stage in front of a live audience. "I'm looking at people's eyes. I am urging them to connect with me. I'm trying to tell you this story. I can scream, I can yell, I can whisper. I can caress with my voice. I can do all of those things, but I want the energy exchange.... And when I can see that it's happening, there's nothing better than that."[89]

If our goal is to build a connection with our audience, we have to show up with the right energy to make that happen—an engaging energy that's aligned with who we are and why we're there. When we don't make the effort, we show up as flat, one-dimensional, or worse, wholly different from who we actually are. This happens a lot in our virtual communication. I had a client who was damaging his connection with his colleagues because of the tone of his posts in their Slack channel. He was dashing off posts to download his opinions or information, without any thought about tone or style and whether they reflected the energy he wanted to bring to their interactions.

Remember the quote from Esther Perel, which is worth repeating—connection is "a vibrational field we can tap into." It's a golden thread that carries energy back and forth between you and your audience. To maximize the power of it, we need to prepare ourselves. Let's start where we always do—with who you are at your core and how powerful that character is. In Chapter 4, you did work to describe how your Power Words show up in your physical presence. Now, it's time to go a little deeper and consider how they'll influence your energy for a specific important interaction.

Translating Your Power Words Into Energy

Start by considering what you know about your audience and why you're the right person to move everybody forward, together, toward a better shared future. Then, define and describe the energy you want to bring to the interaction to make that possible. Consider the following questions:

- How does your core defining word influence how you want to show up?

- What kind of mindset do you want to maintain?

- How do you want your audience to feel while being in your presence?

- Are there any nuances to the situation that influence the energy your audience needs from you?

- What do all of these elements of your energy look like in your body, your expressions, in how you speak?

I had the privilege of studying musical theater performance under the legendary Susan Hight Denny, who starred in the original production of *Guys and Dolls* on Broadway. Now, I can't sing, and Sue told me so. "Pamela, you can't sing, but I can teach you to sell a song." What she meant was to perform it by bringing the full range of my energy and personality to it. That's the gift you can give your audience. And to this day, I still use a technique she gave me personally and with the people I coach.

Sue would tell us that our job onstage was to emanate the rays of our energy from our body out toward the audience so they could bask in the glow of all that we have to offer. She would ask us to close our eyes and imagine standing on stage, in the spotlight, arms raised, energy bursting forth, and thunderous applause rolling back toward us. She didn't know she was teaching a power pose, popularized by Amy Cuddy in her seminal TED Talk and book *Presence*. but it certainly felt like one. With that brief visualization, I would open my eyes and start singing with everything I had. And it worked for me and for my audiences.

Shine Your Rays

Using the work you did in the last exercise to understand how you can translate who you are into the energy you show up with, give yourself a visualization exercise to tap into it. It might not be standing on a stage in a spotlight, but by all means use that if it works for you. What might it look like to successfully shine your rays on the people you communicate with most often? Describe the feeling of connection that comes from that moment for you. Now turn on your camera, dive into that meeting you were dreading with renewed energy, and see what happens.

Overcoming the Biggest Energy Blocker: Fear

After taking the leap from lawyering to acting I immersed myself in classes, and traveled to New York and Oxford, England, to immerse myself in training programs. And yet, through it all, my energy wasn't shining, it was being dimmed. I was afraid—afraid my choice had been a mistake, afraid of getting up in front of "real" actors, afraid of being judged. Fear was my proverbial fourth wall and it was paralyzing me.

Then one day as I was sitting in a hot class room at the Neighborhood Playhouse in New York, the legendary acting teacher Richard Pinter said something that has stuck with me for my whole life. "There's scared and you *do* and scared and you *don't*. You're going to be scared anyway, so you might as well *do*."

Getting up in front of an audience, even an audience of one when the stakes are high or the situation is difficult, creates some level of fear or anxiety for most people. Stage fright is a problem even for professional performers. For anybody, pro or not, standing in front of and trying to connect with people requires a level of vulnerability that can be very uncomfortable. The famous quote often attributed to Rosalind Russell says it all, "Acting is standing up naked and turning around very slowly."

Here's how I ask my most nervous clients to flip the script: Showing up afraid is the most selfish way of showing up. "I'm not selfish!" they always say. "I care deeply about what they think." Yes, you care deeply what they think *about you*. And that's what shows up in your behavior—your focus on yourself—if you can't work past it. Worse, your audience is missing out on the whole wonderful breadth of what you have to offer because when you're in a state of fear, you will hold back.

Talia was a new client who had taken on a huge role as the head of advertising for an iconic consumer brand—and she needed to hear this message more than any other client I've worked with. She had a reputation as a brilliant marketer, but every time she had to speak in front of more than one person, even people she knew well, she became a puddle. She hated it…and it was a big part of her job. It was so bad that when we first met she proudly showed me her big, designer bag of courage, filled with bottles of mood-altering substances to get her through each presentation.

There's a famous story that may or may not be true about the great actor Sarah Bernhardt. When her protégé told Sarah that she didn't get nervous before going on, Sarah said, "Don't worry. It comes with talent." That's a little harsh, but the idea isn't wrong. Anxiety comes from caring, from wanting to get it right, from really wanting to connect. So some anxiety is a good thing. But terror requiring multiple medications? Despite her role and the talent that got her there, there was a huge disconnect between who Talia was at her core and how she was showing up both on and off stage—and the meds weren't helping. I had my work cut out for me, especially since she was scheduled to deliver a speech to an audience of over 10,000 people in just a few months!

When I shared the bit of wisdom with Talia that it was selfish to show up in a state of fear, I saw a light go on behind her eyes, a little understanding that yes, her focus had been on her experience, not on her audience's. "And remember," I told her, "if the goal of being charismatic is to be engaging and interesting, there's nothing more engaging and interesting than a real, honest human being who isn't perfect."

After working through the foundations I've described in earlier chapters and on her archetypes and scripts, Talia and I began to focus on her upcoming speech. We worked through the audience exercise at a high level, given what we knew about the nature of the conference. Then we narrowed in on one specific person that we made up—the person who had shown up at the conference hoping to be in the presence of someone who cared about them, their needs, wants, and future story.

With this understanding of the audience in place, I led her through the next exercise. I've described energy as the golden thread between you and your audience, so one way to overcome fear is to visualize the audience bringing their own amazing energy to the exchange. Then, the stability and integrity of the thread isn't all on you.

The Ideal Audience Energy

As we always do with visualization exercises, sit quietly, silence all your communication devices, relax your body and mind, and get ready to do some imagining. Now, imagine you are walking into the meeting room or onto the stage where you'll be engaging with your audience—whether it's a conversation, a presentation, or a speech. Visualize your audience sitting there anticipating your arrival. As you enter, they quiet down and pay attention to you fully.

As you stand in front of them, imagine being connected to them with a visible thread of energy. You're feeling focused, clear, and confident. See them smiling, sitting up, paying attention (no one is scrolling while you are talking). But don't think about what you will say to them.

Now jump ahead, all the way to the end. You've accomplished the exact outcome you wanted. They've been engaged, influenced, moved by you. It's been a roaring success. Get specific. How specifically has the audience responded to being in your presence? What was their behavior like throughout? At the end? If you're in sales, they've said yes. If you're leading a team meeting, they're on board and ready to take action. If you're coaching someone, their thinking and motivation have shifted.

Give Yourself the Gift of a Mantra

As an actor, I've never experienced anything quite like standing backstage in the dark minutes before the curtain rises, feeling the anticipatory energy of the audience flow off them.

Ask any stage actor and they'll tell you that audiences who come on different days have a unique energy. For me, Wednesday and Thursday night audiences are my favorite. Friday audiences are so tired from the week. And with Saturday night audiences, it all depends on the weather. If it's a nice day, they've spent it outside and active. They come in exhausted, and you've got to rev them up.

But whatever energy they bring, I have to bring my own and manage theirs, by listening and preparing myself for connection. How?

Standing backstage, I take in their energy, I listen to their imagined heartbeats. Researchers have found that theater audience members' heartbeats synch up during live theater performances.[90] Again, we all tap into the vibrational energy of a moment, a shared experience. I feel that energy and then just before the stage manager says, "Places," I repeat my personal mantra. What is it? "I own this room." I use it every time I'm going to step onstage or in front of a room of people waiting to be inspired and entertained and changed on some level.

My mantra doesn't mean what you might think. It's not about me owning the room and the audience *not* owning it. I think of it as owning the room *with* the audience. I feel an energy of play, generosity, and connection in the phrase. I want to own the room for my audience so that they can trust themselves to laugh with abandon, cry if they feel it, and be moved. If I've done my job right, paid attention to them and their needs, and focus on bringing the right energy, I'll have made it safe and comfortable for them to own it with me.

Talia's mantra was, "We are together, for each other." It reminded her why she was there, and she felt supported by the audience. She leveraged it as we prepared and rehearsed. She would say it before visualization exercises, imagining what it would look like for her to bring her true, core self to the stage. And on the last day of rehearsal, when I took her to an empty theater for a dress rehearsal, she said it off stage before walking out and giving it her all. The change I saw in her presence was palpable. More important, though, was how much more secure she felt. "I think I've got this," she said—and I knew she was right.

When the moment came for her to take the stage in front of that 10,000-person strong audience, she strode with confidence to the podium and nailed the performance. She was fully herself in the moment, connecting deeply and believably with her audience.

Your Mantra for Connection

Given what you know about who you are and what kind of energy you want to bring to most interactions, what's something you could say to yourself to reset and focus? What would prepare you to create the golden thread of energy connecting you to your audience?

Now say it out loud. Test it the next time you need to build connection with a person or a group. Shout it to the rafters. And keep saying it until you feel it deepening your connection to who you are at your core and to your audience.

Before your next important conversation, meeting, or presentation, take the time to think deeply about your audience, what they need from you, and the connection you're trying to build with them. Then center yourself, move beyond your fear, listen to their hearts, say your mantra, and go break through that fourth wall!

CHAPTER 12

SHOWTIME! DELIVERING YOUR MESSAGE WITH IMPACT

"That's the magic of art and the magic of theatre. It has the power to transform an audience…and give them an epiphanal experience that changes their life, opens their hearts and their minds and the way they think."[91]—BRIAN STOKES MITCHELL

Zoe was about to guide her team through one of the greatest challenges of the last several decades—the pandemic. As a leader, she had made commitments to be bold and to be a catalyst of growth for her team and her company.

Her team dispersed to their houses and began dealing with the day-to-day challenges of working in isolation while managing family life. And Zoe started reading all the data showing that people across the country were feeling burned out, disconnected, lonely, and stressed. She wanted to alleviate some of those feelings for her team. Of course she wanted them to believe in her leadership during the crisis, but more important, she wanted them to feel connected, seen, and heard, without adding to their growing schedule of Zoom meetings. She wanted to inspire their belief in themselves as they worked through their struggles together.

The previous person in her role had sent out a brief motivational email to the team every Monday. But given that people weren't seeing her as often, and given that she was a natural performer, I suggested that she create lively short videos each week, sharing what the team should focus on, what wins they had had, and what obstacles they needed to overcome together.

"I don't know," she said. "Will anyone watch them? Is this something somebody in my role should do? Isn't it too personal, because I'll have to do it from home?" But the greatest challenge was feeling in the spotlight. Zoe was an only child, and her whole life, everybody had warned her about "only child syndrome"—the perspective that they're the center of the world, the most important person in the room. Zoe's derailer was that she was so worried about becoming that person, she had swung maybe too far in the opposite direction. She had overidealized the servant-leader archetype. She was worried that the videos would be all about her, her own little one-woman show, that she couldn't see the positive impact they could have.

She understood her team needed something from her to feel more connected and to have more moments of inspiration. We talked through why the videos might be the perfect avenue. It took boldness, but she was somebody who was always willing to try new things, so that's what she agreed to do, despite her concerns.

She started with a few nervous recordings from her home office that, honestly, were a bit stilted. I encouraged her to open up, to be more vulnerable, to let people in, to add a little levity. (If she were making them today, I would suggest she watch some of Keanu Reeves's or Jennifer Garner's funny, generous, and genuine short social videos for inspiration.) The next few weeks, she tried recording the videos in different places around her house—the kitchen, the backyard, even her kids' playroom. Initially, she re-recorded them over and over until she felt they were perfect. But eventually, she began to let go and allow them to be human. Each week, she focused on elements of the team's mission. She gave shout outs to individuals to celebrate their successes—and you and I both know the team was watching for those moments. Most important, she listened to the kinds of questions people on the team were asking throughout the week and honed her message to address as many of them as she could.

Soon, she was showing up as her full, wonderful, caring self, with a powerful message every week—and her people loved it! They all watched it. The content helped them feel in the know and more able to focus at a time when things felt chaotic. They got to know their leader, her true character. Even though it was a one-way communication, they felt heard and included. And the next time the company ran its employee engagement survey, Zoe had the highest numbers of anybody on the leadership team.

Your job in life, personally and professionally, is to have a positive, even transformative, impact on the people around you, your community, and the world you're building together. Otherwise, you're just marking time. Whether you're reaching one person or thousands, whether you're communicating in-person or virtually, in writing or on video, you can always make an impact, even if in a small way. That's the goal of all the work in this book, to help you connect with, influence, and inspire other people, as wholly and believably you, so that you can make exciting, positive things happen together and feel confident throughout the journey! Sometimes, to do that, you have to take to the stage—metaphorical or actual—and that can feel risky. A lot of us hold back from this last step. But we can't tell our important stories or advocate for ourselves or others if we aren't willing to step into the spotlight.

One of my favorite scenes in a movie is from *All That Jazz*. In a montage of the famous choreographer and director Bob Fosse (played by Roy Scheider) preparing himself for the day, he looks in the bathroom mirror, gives a quick jazz hands, and says, "Showtime!" The movie was a little dark, but that moment for me is about preparing to show up for the "Showtime! moments" we have every day—opportunities to be who you are, wherever you are, in order to ignite your audience. Whether it's getting your four-year-old to put their shoes on, improving collaboration with a difficult colleague, guiding your team to execute a new plan, or galvanizing thousands to take action, your message and how you deliver it should build connection and excitement about the possibilities of what comes next. It's not hard to do, if you're thoughtful and prepared.

In this final chapter, I'll help you communicate a powerful message, in a way that allows you to believably inspire your audience, in small moments and big. That's how you'll make the biggest impact. If all the world's a stage, you'll discover how to step onto it confidently, advocate for your message, expand your impact, and create more possibilities.

We're Given Opportunities for Impact Every Day

Every time I met with Peter, he would complain that his whole life was just meeting after meeting. "I feel like I spend my days sitting in conference rooms or on Zoom calls. I'm not even sure it even matters what happens in those meetings. I just sit and listen to other people talk."

Which is exactly what his boss told me was one of the problems.

"What's the point of that?" I said. "Each of those meetings is an opportunity for you to make an impact, and you're missing those opportunities."

Peter gave me a raised eyebrow. He had become so cynical about meetings, he was skeptical that anything of value could come from them. The only way to prove the opposite was to get him to try.

When actors are getting into a new script, they sometimes do a little improvisation exercise. They'll run through a scene again and again, and as they read their lines, they'll emphasize different words.

There's NO place like home. There's no place like HOME. There IS no place like home. What they're doing is playing with the impact a certain line can have within the scene, on the other actors (because those points of emphasis might change how those actors deliver their lines), and ultimately on the audience. It's like the story I told in Chapter 9 about my director changing a simple pause in a sentence in my performance of Erma Bombeck to make a stronger impact on the audience. Actors work moment to moment, and the real work is taking advantage of even small opportunities to make an impact in each moment.

Peter and I started to focus on his impact by working through his regular meeting cadence. For each, I asked, "What could you do differently to show up more fully as you and make an impact?" I wanted him to go in feeling more energized. We prepared for even regular, mundane meetings, scouring them for opportunities to contribute in a way that would be helpful to his colleagues. After a couple of weeks, he told me he was starting to get used to the sound of his own voice, which used to make him self-conscious. More important, his contributions were getting noticed and appreciated. In a one-on-one, his director shared the positive things she had been hearing about him from leaders in other departments. Even more important than that, he started to see change happening in the team's processes, in key decisions, and in the work they delivered, based on his contributions. By paying attention to all of his possible "Showtime! moments," no matter how small, he was rewiring believability for himself and for others.

In the rest of the chapter, I'll guide you to being thoughtful and intentional about the impact of your interactions and how to manage your audience's energy, so that you all walk away from a meeting, a presentation, or an important conversation energized and elevated. That's when you'll know you have made an impact.

Align *You* with Your Message

In the last chapter, we focused on your audience and the energy you could bring to your interactions to build a connection with them. Now we have to consider the content of the interaction and how to bring it to life by revealing yourself through it. Remember, people will have a hard time believing what you say or being moved by it if they sense that it's fundamentally misaligned with how you're delivering it, with who you are or who you *say* you are.

Just as you aren't *you* in a vacuum, your message can't be constructed in a vacuum. It needs to convey something beyond basic facts if it's going to support a connection between who you are, why you care, who your audience is, and why they should care.

What's Your Message and Why Does It Matter to You?

"I don't have a message. I have an update. How is that supposed to make an impact?"

I hear something like this from a lot of the people I work with. They don't feel any real connection to what they communicate day in and day out because it's transactional. Instead of a message, they have information to deliver. Or sometimes, bigger messages they have to deliver are handed to them, like when managers need to share a new strategy from the leadership team or a salesperson has to deliver a presentation developed by the marketing team. But here's my question. If you dismiss your personal connection to whatever it is you have to communicate, why should your *audience* feel any connection to it? Why should they even listen?

I'm not saying that every email or hallway conversation has to be a big production, with showtunes and background dancers. But think about it this way: Even delivering a status update can be an opportunity to make an impact and grow your believability. Even if all you have to say is, "Nothing has changed, everything's going to plan," your real message is that you're doing your job well, that your projects are succeeding, that you're giving your colleagues what they need to succeed. And in all of that, your Power Words are probably shining through. So instead of saying, "Nothing has changed, everything's going to plan," you could take a few extra seconds to say, "I'm really proud of my team. They've been consistently delivering excellent work on time." Or, "We had a close call this week, but George in accounting saved the day, we got the materials we needed from a vendor, and we kept the project on track." Or imagine if you took just a moment to truthfully explain why *you* are excited about a new company strategy because of new opportunities it could create for the team. Or imagine how much more engaging your presentation might be if you wove in just two or three mini, two-sentence personal stories that highlight your belief in the ideas.

Imagine how your content and delivery might change with this kind of intentional messaging. And imagine the impact that could have on the other people in the room, how they might pay more attention.

Turning Information Into Impact

- Think about a meeting you have this week and why you're attending. What information do you need to deliver? Or what ideas do you need to share? What big takeaways do you want people to remember?

- Now think about the information, ideas, and takeaways as a message, with more depth and meaning, that you want to convey about the work you're doing.

- Next, consider your Power Words. How do they align with that message? How could you weave them in or allow them to shine through?

- Finally, how can you put this all together and elevate the message for the greatest impact?

Try the next exercise to improve your messaging and how you're revealing who you are through it. Do this intentional work for as many "Showtime! moments" as possible for the next month. Pay attention to how it's changing your communication and how it's changing people's response to you, their perceptions of you. The goal is to shift how you think about these moments so that you're automatically more intentional and consistently more believable, even when you don't have the opportunity to do all of the prep work.

How Will Your Throughline Shine Through?

Remember all that work we did on your throughline—the stories of your past that reveal and support your story of the future? The whole point is to use them to grow your believability and your impact.

I was working with a woman, Sophia, who had built an amazing career in the tech world. She had been hired by a fast-growing AI company and wanted to grow her impact with the rest of the leadership team, the company's stakeholders, and her own team. She often had to give presentations to corporate customers and investors, and she felt like they weren't engaging enough. She shared one that had been recorded with me and I saw the problem right away. No stories, zero personal connection, a missing throughline.

"What they care about is the amazing advances that are happening," she said.

"But so do you, right? If you want to have a bigger impact, you need to show that. You need to leverage your throughline."

She had moved from company to company every seven years or so. "I would rather leave once I've made a contribution and start looking for the next big thing that's on the horizon," she had told me. She was a visionary, a trailblazer, somebody who wanted to keep making a difference. She was always on the hunt for the next big problem and the disruptor companies that were working on solutions that were exciting to her. And every time she moved, the company she moved to hit its mark and changed the world.

Instead of a quick sentence about the companies she had worked for in the past, she needed to share the story of her career in a way that would allow her trailblazer throughline to shine through—because it meant that her current company was a trailblazer too. And that she had the passion and expertise to help it succeed. As great as the technology was that she was "selling," she needed to invite the audience to join her on the journey into a different future.

She started sharing her background as a story, albeit a quick one, and weaving her trailblazer throughline into her presentations. I even told her that I wanted to see it as a theme that showed up in every slide headline. As she connected it to the work her company was doing, her presentations came to life and she started seeing much better results.

Consider a message that you need to communicate often and find the stories that you can leverage to share it with greater impact. They could be your own stories, allowing you to bring who you are to your message, or they could be stories from your team. And remember, stories can be told in a couple of sentences, so you can find opportunities to weave them and your throughline in to almost any communication on any platform, even in a short social post. Use your throughline as one of the greatest conduits you have for connection and impact as you play you and bridge the believability gap.

How Will You Create
Breakthrough Moments?

Zach had to deliver a speech at a major industry conference on how experiences can help brands build connections with their customers. His company was one of the largest experiential marketing agencies in the world and he had a ton of great stories. But he was concerned that he would be just another talking head showing videos and offering his own version of "five points to success." He was also the opening speaker, which meant people's coffee wouldn't have even kicked in yet.

How was he going to create something engaging and impactful?

First, we decided to dig into his message and understand how it aligned with who he was. He quickly realized that his talk was really about creating powerful experiences in unpredictable conditions, or how to turn chaos into delight for audiences while being able to handle all the pitfalls and possibilities along the way. And it was a message so true to Zach, whose character beliefs were creativity, expertise, and adventure.

He was committed to having his audience *experience* his thesis, the idea that from chaos you can build connection. And he wanted them to deeply understand what experiential marketing might feel like in the moment. "So, you have to start by creating chaos and unpredictability?" I asked. And that question opened up a world of possibilities. As we talked about the venue, he explained that it was next to a famous beach. We looked at each other in a eureka moment—beach balls! We could make them play a game of "keepie uppie" with beach balls. It was a great way to create a little safe chaos, get people's pulses going, and capture the unpredictability that comes in his line of work.

He came prepared with about fifteen beach balls and opened his speech by starting to throw them into the audience and asking the group to keep the beach balls in the air for as long as they could. At first people looked at him like he was crazy. Then it got truly chaotic as he threw more beach balls out—a few cups of coffee went flying, people were suddenly lunging into the aisles. But then a rhythm started to emerge. People were paying attention. Energy was mounting. What started as chaos eventually turned into a game filled with squeals of delight and laughter. The entire audience was putting their whole bodies into his presentation. When he finally yelled, "Stop!" they were out of breath, smiling, energized, and connected. And that was a powerful launching point for his message.

Consider this: what's the point of being in a room with another person or group if you're just dryly delivering information they could read in an email. The point in being there *with* them is to bring the message to life through your presence and the experience! In any interaction, you have an opportunity to create what I call "breakthrough moments," like Zach did. It doesn't have to be quite so…chaotic. It might be as simple as asking a targeted and unexpected question right at the start that makes people lean in or take stock. It might be revealing data they've never seen before or in a way that creates a new level of understanding. What could you do for your audience that energizes them, that shifts the tone of the conversation, or that generates "aha!" insights about your message?

It's especially important to think about this question for meetings, especially the ones you have every week or month. Studies and surveys keep reminding us how unproductive team meetings tend to be, how people dread them, how dull and uninspiring they usually are. You can find lots of science-backed solutions for making them better. Personally, I think the greatest challenge is that they become so rote that we don't work at making them exciting, interesting, and engaging. We never consider that they are opportunities to create breakthrough moments, to bolster people's passion and focus.

How are you creating breakthrough moments that leave people clear and committed, whether you're the team leader or somebody on the team who's trying to rally support for your project? Are you telling important stories that get people engaged? Are you creating a moment that primes people's emotional pump or helps them buy in to solving an important problem? Are you fostering humor and laughter? Psychological research has shown that levity improves participation and problem solving and that teams that laugh together perform better, long-term.[92] Are you sharing praise and successes that highlight how you succeed together? Patrick Lencioni recommends using a team rallying cry to get people highly focused on a near-term goal. And if you have team Why and How statements, you should be weaving them into your meetings to build a connection between the work of the moment to the bigger picture.

One note of caution. Take the time to consider your audience and whether your breakthrough moment idea will work for them or create the desired result. Asking the wrong question during a coaching session, for instance, could make the other person shut down instead of engage more. Or if you're working with a group of people, an awkward or uncomfortable experience could get in the way of your message rather than boost it.

I learned this lesson the hard way when facilitating a session with a group of female and male leaders in Saudi Arabia. When he had hired me, the organizer had impressed upon me that I shouldn't change my approach or content. "You be you!" he said, something I'm always happy to hear. I felt comfortable with his advice, but I did consider my attire carefully and I adjusted my humor a bit to align with the local culture.

The program was going well and the audience was engaged. And then I had them stand up and get ready for an exercise I had done loads of times in the past. Everyone forms two lines, facing each other. One side is given cards with emotions on them and the other side has to guess what the person is "feeling" just by watching their faces for one minute. The goal is to help people understand empathy and how we can read people's emotions when we pay attention and look them in the eye.

We'll have some breakthrough moments for sure, I thought. Well, we did, but they were all mine. The exercise fell flat. It was truly uncomfortable for some of them to look each other in the eye for deeply rooted cultural reasons.

Not all ideas for creating breakthrough moments are ideal for all audiences, so always start there. Remember, having an impact is the whole point of breakthrough moments to begin with—and you want it to be a positive one.

How Will Your Impact Extend Beyond the Interaction?

Impact isn't true impact if it doesn't last longer than a conversation or a speech. And one of the great challenges of any communication is impacting what happens next. Too often, you share your message and people seem interested, engaged, on board, or at least not openly hostile to your ideas. You walk away feeling like you've succeeded. And then…nothing changes. If you're a parent, you probably experience this a lot.

Typically, you want your audience to do something after your interaction. It could be as simple as taking out the garbage, as mundane as sending an email with more information, as important as signing a contract, or as complex as changing their habits. Before every moment of possible impact, ask yourself first, Do I know exactly what I want people to do next? Do I know what support I need or that my team or community needs to make progress? Because if you aren't sure, they won't be either and they won't take action.

Once you do know, consider how to communicate a persuasive and energizing call to action. One powerful tool, as always, is story. I described Marshall Ganz's Story of Self in Part 2 and Story of Us in Part 3. Now we can turn to his Story of Now. Ganz defines the Story of Now as the urgent challenge you face and the threat to the values you share with your audience that demands immediate action, paired with a picture of what the future will look like if you act now—or if you don't. Even in smaller moments of impact, you can use the Story of Now to connect current action to a better, inspiring future. How can you encourage your audience by telling a story of what the future will look like if they take action?

The bigger question is, Are you making them feel integral to what comes next, a part of the journey, clear on their role and passionate about bringing their greatest attributes to it? Because that connection is how you can believably expand your impact.

Crafting Your Call to Action
and Story of Now

- What do you need or want your audience to do, specifically, based on your message?

- What are some shared values that you could weave in to get them engaged and excited about supporting you?

- How can you tell a brief story of the future that's collective, about you and them, that helps them understand the benefit of taking action? It could be as brief as a sentence or two.

- Do you have a story from the past that illustrates that imagined future? Everything you want to do you have done in some form or other in the past, and it can guide you toward your imagined future.

- To persuade them, do you need to contrast your positive story with a narrative of what the future will look like if nobody takes action?

- How can you encourage them to bring their true selves to the challenge or the situation? Why will their specific action will be meaningful because of who they are and their unique attributes?

How Will Your Audience Be Changed by You?

The best moments of communication are a dialogue—even when the other person or group doesn't talk. They can still be fully in it with you. And you know that they are when they're reacting—with nods, smiles, or my favorite, laughter. You start by reaching their ears (auditory), you may reach them with beautiful images or slides (visual), but then you have to reach their heart (emotional). That's when you've made a real, *lasting* impact on your audience.

When you are preparing to speak up at a meeting or stand on a stage, ask yourself, How can I reach them, on every level? How can I change their perspective? How can I help them walk away positively changed from being in my presence? And most important, how can I make them feel something—about themselves, about me, about the deeper message and mission I'm here to talk about?

Because that's the path to genuine, believability-building influence, connection, and impact.

COMMIT TO YOUR BEST ROLE EVER—
YOU!

Every time an actor steps onto the stage or onto a set, it's an act of courage. It takes a leap of faith, and the only way they can take the leap over and over again is by committing to their character and dedicating themselves to performing their role to the best of their abilities. They have to work at becoming masters of their craft, which is work that never, ever ends.

It's no different for any of us. Think about the courage it takes to be vulnerable and ask a person or a team for their support, to share a very different vision of the future, to share a bold idea for how to work better together, to ask for what we need with calm confidence, to step up into a leadership role for the first time, to see yourself as a leader no matter your role, to support somebody by challenging them to grow.

Showing up as your whole wonderful self, day in and day out, to achieve what you want in your work and life takes courage. Remember what the great communicator Edward R. Murrow said. "To be persuasive, we must be believable; to be believable we must be credible; to be credible we must be truthful."[93] If you don't maintain your commitment to your character and your dedication to bringing your whole, truthful self to the role of the moment, the courage you need to close the believability gap can slip away. The gap widens as you start hiding or suppressing essential elements of who you are at your core and your essential stories. Then your archetypes and scripts start to take over, and building connection and impact becomes so much harder.

I was a few weeks into a coaching engagement with a client when she said to me, "But when are we going to work on my confidence?"

"What do you mean?" I said. "That's all we've been working on!"

The problem was, she wasn't bringing our work into her daily experiences. She wasn't committing to her character in big and small moments, leveraging it as a source of power, connection, and impact. To overcome the knowing-doing gap that gets in the way of personal growth, before you put this book down, I encourage you to do the following:

- ★ If you haven't already, put your Power Words on a Post-it note—maybe more than one—to remind yourself who you're trying to bring to life in any moment.

- ★ Answer this question: What are three things I'm going to start doing or stop doing that will help me play me more consistently and completely? Consider your problematic archetypes and scripts that will get in the way if you give them room. What can you do to override them? Where in your life do you feel like you're still holding back? Be specific. List actions you'll take and habits you'll build. Don't overdo it. Start with three. When those three become easy, do the exercise again.

- ★ Every day, take a couple of minutes to remind yourself why you're doing this courageous work. Try journaling at the end of the day about what you learned about your character, where you're showing up believably, or where you aren't. Try a visualization exercise, focusing on the future story you're trying to create. Or just think about one of the best days of the last week or month and how it felt to bring all of you to a challenge or opportunity.

These simple actions can help you close the believability gap whenever and wherever it shows up for you. It's the few cues you need to remind you who you are, what you're working toward, and how you want to show up—like cue cards or a pivotal line an actor writes on their hand so they can nail it when they're in the moment.

You don't know what role will come your way next, in your work and in your life, or what opportunity you'll have to fulfill your Why or your How, your purpose or your mission. When I was offered the role of Erma Bombeck, I was already overflowing with work in my professional life. But I have such deep admiration for her humor, her courage, her vulnerability, and her outsized generosity and warmth, I just had to accept the role. And I'm so thankful I did. Playing her helped me reconnect with who I am at my core and find a new way to fulfill my Why—to share my energy with the world. There's a line toward the end of the play, based on words she actually said, that captures so much of who she was, what I want for my life, and what I hope for you. "When I stood before Him at the end of my life, I didn't want to have a single bit of energy or talent left. My plan was to wear out, not rust out. I look forward to saying, 'I used everything you gave me.' But most of all, given another shot at life, I would seize every minute to make a difference."[94]

The more committed you are to your character, the more prepared you'll be to let it shine through. Give yourself the tools and foundation to achieve that wonderful state of living truthfully in your given circumstances. And then get out there, step into the spotlight, and persuasively, believably, credibly, confidently play the role of a lifetime—You.

MORE HELP ALONG YOUR JOURNEY

My mission is to help you believably present yourself, your ideas, and your stories to grow your confidence, connection, and impact. This book offers a template that allows you to create your own journey to those goals. Embedded in each chapter are multiple exercises to help you along—do them!

But for even more support on your journey, you can turn to my website, ThePamSherman.com, where you can

* Find more exercises and user-friendly versions of exercises in this book
* Access virtual coaching, nudging you to bring your character alive in your day-to-day work and life
* Sign up for my monthly newsletter for more insights and stories
* Reach out to me for personalized help for you, your team, your organization, or your members, based on my proprietary EDGE: Explore, Dream, Grow & Excite programs

And I would love to hear from you about how this book has helped, especially stories of how you've bridged the believability gap. Or take a photo of your Power Words on a Post-it note and email it to me or share it with me via social. I love building a community of people trying to generously bring who they are to the world!

ENDNOTES

1   Edward R. Murrow, speaking to Congress, while acting as director of the United States Information Agency, May 1963.

2   "What Is the Meisner Technique," Meisner Technique Studio, accessed September 30, 2025, https://themeisnertechniquestudio.com/meisner-technique/

3   Patricia Faison Hewlin, "How to Be More Authentic at Work," *Greater Good,* August 3, 2020. https://greatergood.berkeley.edu/article/item/how_to_be_more_authentic_at_work

4   "Survey of over 52,000 workers indicates the Great Resignation is set to continue as pressure on pay mounts," PwC.com, May 24, 2022. www.pwc.com/gx/en/news-room/press-releases/2022/global-workforce-hopes-and-fears-survey-2022.html

5   Geoff Colvin, *Humans Are Underrated* (Portfolio, New York, 2015), 53.

6   Bryan Cranston, *A Life in Parts,* (Scribner, New York, 2016), 199.

7   "Hilary Swank | In Conversation With…| TIFF 2018," TIFF Originals, YouTube, September 18, 2018. https://www.youtube.com/watch?v=NF1VARbZI74&t=3077s

8   Rebecca Leung, "Hilary Swank: Oscar Gold," CBS News, August 12, 2005, https://www.cbsnews.com/news/hilary-swank-oscar-gold-12-08-2005/

9   Caroline McHugh, "The Art of Being Yourself," TEDxMiltonKeynesWomen, TEDx Talks, YouTube, February 15, 2013. www.youtube.com/watch?v=veEQQ-N9xWU

10 Brian Goldman and Michael Kernis, "Role of Authenticity in Healthy Psychological Functioning and Subjective Well-Being," *Annals of the American Psychotherapy Association,* November-December 2002. https://psycnet.apa.org/record/2002-11420-003

11 Jay Shetty, *Think Like a Monk* (Simon & Schuster, New York, 2020), 3–4.

12 Mark Manson, "Personal Values: How to Know Who You Really Are," *Mark Manson* (blog), May 20, 2025. https://markmanson.net/personal-values

13 Daniel Pink, *Drive* (Riverhead Books, New York 2009), 132.

14 William Damon, Jenni Menon, and Kendall Cotton Bronk, "The Development of Purpose During Adolescence," *Applied Developmental Science,* Vol. 7, No 3, 2003. https://kremen.fresnostate.edu/centers-.projects/bonnercenter/documents/Development.pdf

15 Heather Malin, Emily Morton, Amber Nadal, Krystal Ann Smith, "Purpose and coping with adversity: A repeated measures, mixed-methods study with

young adolescents," *Journal of Adolescence,* Vol. 76, October 2019. https://www.sciencedirect.com/science/article/abs/pii/S0140197119301290#!

16 Patrick Hill, Anthony Burrow, Kendall Cotton Bronk, "Persevering with Positivity and Purpose: An Examination of Purpose Commitment and Positive Affect as Predictors of Grit," *Journal of Happiness Studies,* Vol. 17, No. 1, November, 2014. https://www.researchgate.net/publication/280568975_Persevering_with_Positivity_and_Purpose_An_Examination_of_Purpose_Commitment_and_Positive_Affect_as_Predictors_of_Grit

17 Adrienne Crowell, Elizabeth Page-Gould, Brandon Schmeichel, "Self-affirmation breaks the link between the behavioral inhibition system and the threat-potentiated startle response," *Emotion,* Volume 15, No. 2, April 2015. https://pubmed.ncbi.nlm.nih.gov/25603136/

18 Elaine Page, "Character Development: A Guide for Actors," *Backstage,* October 17, 2023. https://www.backstage.com/magazine/article/character-development-for-actors-76083/

19 Adam Grant, *Originals* (Penguin Random House, New York, 2016), 13–14.

20 Bartleby, "How to Inspire People," *The Economist,* December 5, 2024. https://www.economist.com/business/2024/12/05/how-to-inspire-people

21 Hidden Brain Staff, "Dropping the Mask," *Hidden Brain,* hosted by Shankar Vedantam, March 3, 2025. https://hiddenbrain.org/podcast/dropping-the-mask

22 Deloitte, "Uncovering Culture: A Call to Action for Leaders," Meltzer Center for Diversity, Inclusion, and Belonging, 2024.

23 Brené Brown, *The Gifts of Imperfection,* 10th Anniversary Edition (Random House, New York, 2020), 37.

24 Ryan Gilbey, "All-Action Heroine," *The Guardian,* December 31, 2008. https://www.theguardian.com/film/2009/jan/01/bond-girl-michelle-yeoh

25 Albert Mehrabian, *Silent Messages* (Wadsworth Publishing Company, Belmont, CA, 1972).

26 Amy Cuddy, *Presence* (Little Brown and Company, New York, 2015), 24.

27 "Andie MacDowell on the Controversy Around 'Greystoke: The Legend Of Tarzan,'" SiriusXM, YouTube, August 25, 2019. https://www.youtube.com/watch?v=6_wyHEXYAHc

28 Xin Wang, et al, "Audio Mining: The Role of Vocal Tone in Persuasion," *Journal of Consumer Research,* Vol. 48, Issue 2, 2021. https://academic.oup.com/jcr/article-abstract/48/2/189/6147021?login=false

29 Annett Schirmer, "Mark My Words: Tone of Voice Changes Affective Word Representations in Memory," *PLoS One, Vol. 5, No. 2, February 15, 2010. https://pmc.ncbi.nlm.nih.gov/articles/PMC2821399/*

30 James Nestor, *Breath* (Riverhead Books, New York, 2020), xix.

31 Alex Lickerman, M.D., "The Importance of Tone," *Psychology Today,* August 5, 2010. https://www.psychologytoday.com/us/blog/happiness-in-this-world/201008/the-importance-of-tone

32 Dalya Alberge, "Sir Derek Jacobi: 'The sound and magic of voice are disappearing from theatre,'" *The Guardian,* March 18, 2023. https://www.theguardian.com/stage/2023/mar/18/derek-jacobi-the-sound-and-magic-of-voice-disappearing-from-theatre

33 Laila Worrell, "Life's Work: An Interview with Viola Davis," *Harvard Business Review,* November-December 2023. https://hbr.org/2023/11/lifes-work-an-interview-with-viola-davis

34 David Brancaccio, "What's the Future of the American Dream," *Marketplace,* August 22, 2016. https://www.marketplace.org/2016/08/22/future-american-dream-secretary/

35 "Interview with Amina Laraki Slaoui," interviewed by Geoffrey Jones, Marrakech, Morocco and Boston, MA, June 14, 2023, Creating Emerging Markets Oral History Collection, Baker Library Special Collections and Archives, Harvard Business School. https://www.hbs.edu/creating-emerging-markets/Documents/transcripts/Amina%20Laraki%20Slaoui_Transcript%20for%20Web.pdf

36 Brian Ackley, "How Actors Help Make Your Script Better," *ScreenCraft,* April 13, 2016. https://screencraft.org/blog/how-actors-help-make-your-script-better/

37 "How to Create a Character with Samuel L. Jackson | Discover MasterClass," MasterClass, YouTube, April 19, 2019. https://www.youtube.com/watch?v=ZOcZ-aT07Cw

38 Laura A. King and Courtney Raspin, "Lost and found possible selves, subjective well-being, and ego development in divorced women," *Journal of Personality,* June 7, 2004. https://pubmed.ncbi.nlm.nih.gov/15102040/ See also: Laura A. King and Camille Patterson, "Reconstructing Life Goals After the Birth of a Child With Down Syndrome: Finding Happiness and Growing," *International Journal of Rehabilitation and Health,* January, 2000. https://link.springer.com/article/10.1023/A:1012955018489

39 Chip Heath and Dan Heath, *Switch* (Broadway Books, New York, 2010), 81.

40 Peter Senge, *The Fifth Discipline* (Crown Currency, New York, 2023), 139–142.

41 The future-self exercise has been described and adapted by a number of other authors, including Henry Kimsey-House et al, in *Co-Active Coaching* (Nicholas Brealey, Boston, 2018).

42 "Colin Farrell: 'I Don't Think Parenthood Changes You,'" *The Talks.* https://the-talks.com/interview/colin-farrell/

43 Julian Voigt, Kennon Sheldon, and Hugo Kehr, "When Visions Truly Inspire: The moderating role of self-concordance in boosting positive affect, goal commitment, and goal progress," *Journal of Research in Personality,* April 2024. https://www.sciencedirect.com/science/article/pii/S0092656624000199

44 Paul J. Zak, "Why Your Brain Loves Good Storytelling," *Harvard Business Review,* October 28, 2014. https://hbr.org/2014/10/why-your-brain-loves-good-storytelling

45 Angus Fletcher, *Storythinking* (Columbia University Press, New York, 2023), 4–5.

46   Annette Simmons, *The Story Factor* (Basic Books, New York, 2000), 3.

47   Constantin Stanislavski, *An Actor Prepares,* Translated by Elizabeth Reynolds Hapgood (Eyre Methuen, London, 1980, paperback edition), 273–274.

48   Tasha Eurich, *Insight,* (Crown Business, New York, 2017), 146.

49   "Viola Davis on Acting," BAFTA Guru, YouTube, February 1, 2017, https://www.youtube.com/watch?v=a-f4DDnGSBc

50   Jazmine Hughes, "Viola Davis, Inside Out," *New York Times,* April 12, 2022. https://www.nytimes.com/2022/04/12/magazine/viola-davis.html

51   "Marshall Ganz Quotes and Wisdom about Leadership, Hope, Organizing and Narrative," The Commons Social Change Library. https://commonslibrary.org/marshall-ganz-quotes-and-wisdom/

52   Dan McAdams, "The Life Story Interview II," Northwestern University, 2007. https://cpb-us-e1.wpmucdn.com/sites.northwestern.edu/dist/4/3901/files/2020/11/The-Life-Story-Interview-II-2007.pdf

53   "Rami Malek: 'It Was Daunting to Live Up to That," *The Talks.* https://the-talks.com/interview/rami-malek/

54   Annette Simmons, *Whoever Tells the Best Story Wins* (AMACOM, New York, 2007), 19.

55   Greg J. Stephens, Lauren J. Silbert, Uri Hasson, "Speaker–listener neural coupling underlies successful communication," *Proceedings of the National Academy of Sciences,* August 10, 2010. https://pubmed.ncbi.nlm.nih.gov/20660768/

56   Melanie Green, "Narratives and Cancer Communication," *Journal of Communication,* August 4, 2026, https://onlinelibrary.wiley.com/doi/abs/10.1111/j.1460-2466.2006.00288.x

57   Karen Eber, *The Perfect Story* (Harper Horizon, 2023), 47.

58   "LeVar Burton Teaches the Power of Storytelling | Official Trailer | MasterClass," YouTube, June 22, 2021. https://www.youtube.com/watch?v=i3U1q25VAaA

59   Mark Twain, speech to the Society of the Army of the Tennessee, November, 12 1879, Thirteenth Annual Report of the Proceedings of the Society of the Army of the Tennessee, (published in a multi-volume set by the society in Cincinnati, 1885).

60   Gilda Radner, *It's Always Something,* 20th anniv. ed., (Simon and Schuster, New York, 2009), 139.

61   Craig Pearce and Hee Man Park, "Are you an accidental dictator?: The smart person leadership trap…and how to avoid it," *Organizational Dynamics,* September 2025. https://doi.org/10.1016/j.orgdyn.2025.101130

62   "Who gets the most *useless* feedback at work," Textio. https://textio.com/feedback-bias-2024

63 Susan Sorenson, "How Employees' Strengths Make Your Company Stronger," Gallup. https://www.gallup.com/workplace/231605/employees-strengths-company-stronger.aspx.

64 Oliver Glass, et al, "Expressive writing to improve resilience to trauma: A clinical feasibility trial," *Complementary Therapies in Clinical Practice*, 2019. https://cssh.northeastern.edu/pandemic-teaching-initiative/wp-content/uploads/sites/43/2020/10/GlassetalTraumaResilience.pdf. See also: Karen Baikie and Kay Wilhelm, "Emotional and physical health benefits of expressive writing," *Advances in Psychiatric Treatment*, 2005. https://doi.org/10.1192/apt.11.5.338

65 "Taylor Russell discusses 'Bones and All,'" Hammer Museum, YouTube, December 15, 2022. https://www.youtube.com/watch?v=I2Rt8z8qNro

66 This article offers a great summary of the extensive research on the benefits of mindfulness practices: Matthew Thorpe and Rachael Ajmera, "How Meditation Benefits Your Mind and Body," *Healthline*, August 15, 2024. https://www.healthline.com/nutrition/12-benefits-of-meditation

67 Epictetus, *Discourses and Selected Writings*, Translated by Robert Dobbin (Penguin Classics, New York, 2008) Book 1, Chapter 18.

68 Katy Milkman, *How to Change* (Penguin, New York, 2021), 141.

69 Andrew Bloomenthal, "Interview: Greta Gerwig, Writer and Director of Lady Bird," *Script*, November 27, 2017. https://scriptmag.com/features/interview-greta-gerwig-writer-director-lady-bird

70 Spence D. "Interview with Joe Pantoliano (Part 1 of 2)," *IGN*, March 31, 2001. https://www.ign.com/articles/2001/03/31/interview-with-joe-pantoliano-part-1-of-2

71 David Novak, *How Leaders Learn* (Harvard Business Review Press, Boston, 2024), 133.

72 Beth Schmid, "Darden's Freeman Teaches Leadership Through J-Term Theater Class," *UVAToday*, University of Virginia, January 12, 2010. https://news.virginia.edu/content/dardens-freeman-teaches-leadership-through-j-term-theater-class

73 Amy Edmondson, "Psychological Safety and Learning Behavior in Work Teams," *Administrative Science Quarterly*, Vol. 44, No. 2, June, 1999. https://www.jstor.org/stable/2666999

74 Ron Friedman, "5 Things High-Performing Teams Do Differently," *Harvard Business Review*, October 21, 2021. https://hbr.org/2021/10/5-things-high-performing-teams-do-differently

75 Jim Asplund, "On the Best Teams, People Know What Makes Each Person Unique," Gallup, October 6, 2022. https://www.gallup.com/cliftonstrengths/en/402578/best-teams-people-know-makes-person-unique.aspx

76 Jack Zenger and Joseph Folkman, "The 3 Elements of Trust," *Harvard Business Review*, February 5, 2019. https://hbr.org/2019/02/the-3-ele-

ments-of-trust See also: Michael Platt and Elizabeth Johnson, "How to Use Neuroscience to Build Team Chemistry," *Knowledge at Wharton,* January 23, 2023. https://knowledge.wharton.upenn.edu/article/how-to-use-neuroscience-to-build-team-chemistry/

77 Nathaniel Lambert, et al, "Benefits of expressing gratitude: expressing gratitude to a partner changes one's view of the relationship," *Psychological Science,* April, 2010. https://pubmed.ncbi.nlm.nih.gov/20424104/

78 Novak, *How Leaders Learn,* 231.

79 "Sam Mendes on his Rehearsal Process | National Theatre," YouTube, May 30, 2014. https://www.youtube.com/watch?v=JevThnO92_c

80 Calum Marsh, "How Chris Messina Forced Matt Damon to Up His Game in 'Air,'" *New York Times,* May 12, 2023. https://www.nytimes.com/2023/05/12/movies/chris-messina-air.html?smid=nytcore-ios-share&referringSource=articleShare

81 Leading Change Network, et al, "The Power of Story: The Story of Self, Us, and Now," The Commons Social Change Library, https://commonslibrary.org/the-power-of-story-the-story-of-self-us-and-now/

82 Kate Stinchfield, "10 Questions for Glenn Close," *Time,* June 28, 2017. https://content.time.com/time/subscriber/article/0,33009,1638431,00.html

83 Patrick Heidmann, "Christoph Waltz: 'It Has Nothing to Do with the Job,'" *The Talks,* https://the-talks.com/interview/christoph-waltz/

84 Kim Mills, host, "Speaking of Psychology: The psychology of sports fans, with Daniel Wann, PhD," American Psychological Association, April 24, 2024. https://www.apa.org/news/podcasts/speaking-of-psychology/sports-fans

85 Rudiger Sturm, "Brie Larsen: 'I Hope My Work Makes People Feel Less Alone,'" *The Talks.* https://the-talks.com/interview/brie-larson/

86 Maria Stavraki, et al, "The influence of emotions on information processing and persuasion: A differential appraisals perspective," *Journal of Experimental Social Psychology,* March, 2021. https://www.sciencedirect.com/science/article/abs/pii/S002210312030425X

87 Esther Perel and Mary Alice Miller, "Letters from Esther #64: Searching for Connection in a Disconnected Era,"estherperel.com. https://www.estherperel.com/blog/letters-from-esther-64-searching-for-connection-in-a-disconnected-era

88 Craig Byrd, "Brian Stokes Mitchell and the LA Phil Take You on a Sonic Ride Through Broadway With In Character," *Cultural Attaché,* February 3, 2016. https://culturalattache.co/2016/02/03/brian-stokes-mitchell-and-the-la-phil-take-you-on-a-sonic-ride-through-broadway-with-in-character/

89 Cynthia Erivo, "Armchair Expert with Dax Shepard," Wondery, November 18, 2024. https://wondery.com/shows/armchair-expert-with-dax-shepard/episode/16193-cynthia-erivo/?queryID=6c65e32ff71018a3416e-7a2014ea2aea

90   "Audience members' hearts beat together at the theatre," University College London. https://www.ucl.ac.uk/brain-sciences/news/2017/nov/audience-members-hearts-beat-together-theatre

91   Craig Byrd, "Brian Stokes Mitchell and the LA Phil Take You on a Sonic Ride Through Broadway With In Character," *Cultural Attaché*, February 3, 2016. https://culturalattache.co/2016/02/03/brian-stokes-mitchell-and-the-la-phil-take-you-on-a-sonic-ride-through-broadway-with-in-character/

92   "Psychological Science Can Make Your Meetings Better," Association for Psychological Science, November 9, 2018. https://www.psychologicalscience.org/news/releases/psychological-science-can-make-your-meetings-better.html

93   Edward R. Murrow, speaking to Congress, while acting as director of the United States Information Agency, May 1963.

94   Allison Engel and Margaret Engel, *Erma Bombeck: At Wit's End* (Samuel French, 2016) 35.

ACKNOWLEDGMENTS

I am someone who believes that if you state a dream out loud you have to follow through on it and make it a reality. When I stated my dream of writing a book about my work in 2015, at a charity luncheon where I met my agent, Michael Palgon, I didn't realize how long it would take to do it. But this book is the book of my dreams, because of the impact I believe it can have on people's personal and professional lives. And it wouldn't have become a reality without the support of the many people who believed in me, stuck with me, were patient with me, pushed me, and shared who they are with me.

Thank you to all who encouraged my storytelling, including my agent, Michael. Thanks to my editor Mark Liu at the *Democrat & Chronicle* who patiently taught me how to be a better writer and helped me be more specific in my storytelling. Big thanks to my collaborators in all the creative stories I share as an actor, including and most especially my original playwrighting collaborator, Caleen Sinnette Jennings; Mark Cuddy, my director and producing partner on *Erma Bombeck: At Wit's End*; and Margaret and Allison Engel, our playwrights, who made my Erma Bombeck journey come to life.

Thanks to my creative content partner, Sheila Dunne, who has helped bolster my online believability. And to Sheila Parr, who has created a cover for this book that truthfully, engagingly reflects what it's all about and my energy for potential readers. Thank you to the editors who helped refine aspects of the content, including Sarah Welch and Samantha Rose. And thank you to Aleigha Koss, my sherpa through the publishing process.

And a most special thanks to Lari Bishop, my collaborator and editor, who shaped my work, my ideas, and my stories into this book with patience, grace, and wisdom.

A shout-out to all my friends and colleagues, who have listened to my dream over and over and over, including and especially: Meg Mundy, Julie Nusbaum, Sue Patrick, Shauna Hicks, Jessica Birnbaum, Mary Tucker, Laura Rebell Gross, Kim Weinberg, Sherre Hirsch, Karen Eber, Erica Keswin, Michelle Carlson, my YPO Forum and friends around the world (and if I forgot you I mean you, too).

And to all those who helped me move my own obstacles to write this book: Kathleen Stetson, Shoshanna Hecht, Becky Cole, William Kenower and especially Joanne Pedro Caroll who has helped me be the best version of me in the world.

Massive gratitude to all the clients I have had the privilege to serve around the world. Those clients who shared their stories and did the work. Those clients who trusted me and who shared their hearts with me to grow and make a greater impact with who they are.

Very special thanks and love to my family—my husband, partner, and fellow dreamer of over forty-three years, Neal Sherman, and our kids, Zach and Eliza, who are now grown-ups. And of course, to our puppies Moe and Allie, who sit at my feet expectantly as I work and write. You are all my test audience and my ultimate improv team. You help ground me, elevate me, and call me on my believability gaps. You have grown my heart and bring joy to my world. Most important you are the embodiment of believability with how you show up in the world for each other and those you impact, lead, and serve.

Finally, thank you to my community for believing in me as I play me. I can't wait to watch you all soar as you play you and build believability bridges that will impact the world.

ABOUT THE AUTHOR

Pam Sherman is an author, speaker, leadership and communication consultant, executive coach, and recovering corporate attorney whose story of ditching that day job to pursue her dream of acting was featured in *People* magazine.

Today, Pam combines her business background with her creative talents to lead group and individual development programs for Fortune 50 companies, nonprofits, and business associations around the world, from Milwaukee to Morocco, New York to Nigeria. She helps people present themselves, their ideas, their organizations with clarity and passion, and bring their amazing, true selves to their communication and collaboration through her proprietary EDGE program. She's a highly rated resource for global leadership organizations, including YPO and Entrepreneurs' Organization (EO).

Pam has performed on stage and in film and television, including *Shear Madness* at the Kennedy Center and *Homicide: Life on the Street.* Her portrayal of Erma Bombeck in *Erma Bombeck: At Wit's End* has played to sold-out audiences around the country. Pam's nationally syndicated column, "The Suburban Outlaw," ran for fifteen years. She was named Humorist of the Month by the Erma Bombeck Writer's Center, and her book, *The Suburban Outlaw*, is a collection of her essays.

In recognition of her work and community contributions, Pam has been honored as an Athena Award Finalist, a Business Journal Woman of Excellence, and a Woman to Watch by Jewish Women International.

Pam lives with her patient husband and two neurotic dogs in Rochester, New York, where she raised two amazing humans, Eliza and Zach.

You can connect with Pam on social platforms—@thepamsherman—and especially on LinkedIn (@pam-sherman). You can subscribe to her newsletter or get in touch via her website, where she offers helpful resources.

ThePamSherman.com